JavaScript Coding for Teens

JavaScript CODING FOR TEENS

A Beginner's Guide to Developing Websites and Games

ANDREW YUEH

Illustrations by Carl Wein

ROCKRIDGE
PRESS

I dedicate this book to Frank and
May Yueh for supporting me during
my transition to a career in coding.

Interior and Cover Designer: Lisa Schreiber
Art Producer: Janice Ackerman
Editor: Andrea Leptinsky
Production Manager: Martin Worthington

Illustrations ©2021 Carl Wein

Paperback ISBN: 978-1-64876-111-9
eBook ISBN: 978-1-64876-112-6
R0

Contents

CHAPTER 10: **Game Time** 133

CHAPTER 11: **Last Stop: Website Upgrades** 157

ANSWER KEY 169

Introduction

Hey there, my name is Andrew Yueh. I'm a hobbyist programmer and professional software developer. Building products that people use and solving technical challenges are my favorite things about programming. My programming language of choice in my professional and personal life is JavaScript.

We are here to get your feet wet in the world of JavaScript and programming fundamentals. Chapters 1 and 2 cover what programming is and how to get your computer ready for JavaScript programming. Chapters 3 through 9 are where the real learning starts. These chapters teach the basics of a variety of core programming concepts.

Each chapter covers a particular coding topic and provides various extra learning and easy reference materials, including an overview of what was covered, an activity, practice problems, and the repair of some sample broken code!

By the end of this book, you will be fully equipped to tackle two fun and challenging projects! Excited to get your hands dirty and wrangle some real code? How does a game sound? Want to get a taste of what it means to be a web developer? You'll take a website and spruce it up!

For extra guidance, we'll be sprinkling some bonus tips, called Hacker Hints, along the way. A glossary at the end of this book allows for easy future reference of common industry terms. Looking to supplement your learning? Good, because we also provide a list of extra resources to check out. Let's get started!

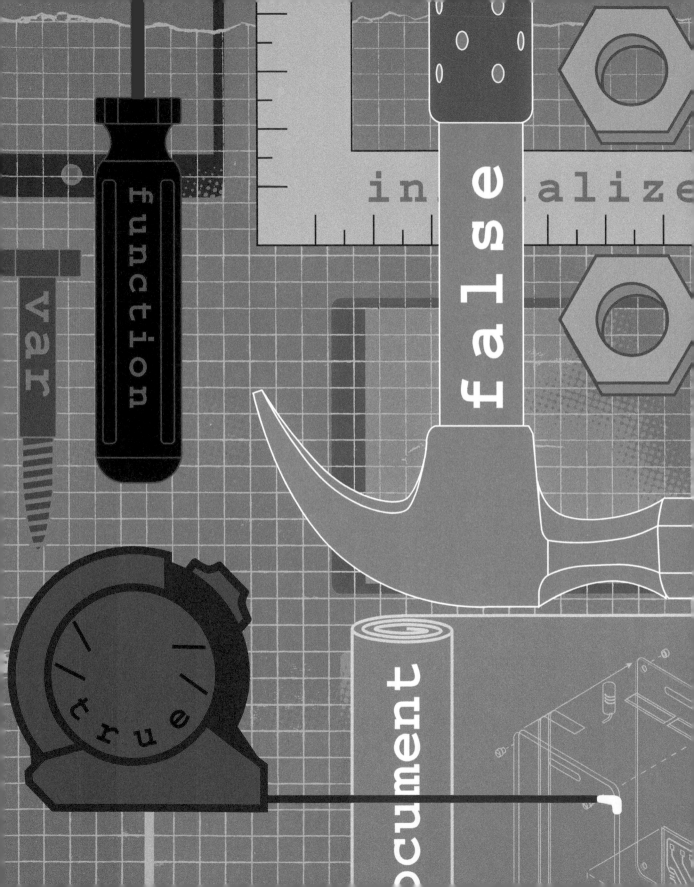

CHAPTER 1

Welcome to Programming in JavaScript

Programming is the art of combining human creativity with raw logic that a computer can understand. The latter is the true challenge. You have spent your entire life thinking like a human, but programming asks you to think like a computer. That may sound difficult, but you can do this. And I'm here to help! Programming helps solve problems that are impossible to solve with other methods. It can perform complex computations, automate processes, and accomplish tasks that the human brain alone cannot handle.

A programming language is a specific tool for translating human instructions to something a computer can interpret. There are many languages out there, and they all have their strengths and weaknesses. But at the end of the day, they all do the same thing: They talk to computers. For this book, the programming language of choice will be JavaScript.

Why JavaScript?

JavaScript is a programming language that was originally made for developing websites. More than 90 percent of the web is powered by JavaScript. Its application has grown far and wide from its original use. JavaScript is now one of the hottest languages to learn.

JavaScript is also a great entry point for any aspiring programmer. Many programming languages require deep understanding of how computers work. JavaScript, on the other hand, handles many of the nitty-gritty details for you.

What Are Programs?

Code improves modern life by solving problems. A **program** is a collection of code that performs or solves a complete idea. The concept of a complete idea is very open ended. Programs come in all shapes, sizes, and uses. They are all around us. I'm sure you already know many programs that you use in your daily life. Do these look familiar?

→ Operating systems like Windows and macOS
→ Mobile apps
→ Web browsers

The world revolves around code. A majority of the programs we use work in the background. What controls the electricity in your neighborhood's power grid? What does an automobile use to control power steering? How is it possible to rub the surface of a phone to access funny cat pictures? These modern feats are possible through the creation and utilization of programs.

Are Websites Computer Programs?

The first websites were not computer programs. But an overwhelming majority of modern ones are. A very brief recap of the history of the Web will explain why.

HTML

The creation of hypertext markup language, referred to as **HTML**, marked the start of communicating visual content on a web browser. These first websites were shockingly boring. They contained no special fonts, colors, or animations. HTML is simply "stuff." Stuff that is not dynamic in any sense of the word. Nothing but plain text, images, and clickable links. In that sense, they were not programs.

Yes, the "L" in HTML stands for "language." But HTML is not a programming language. It is a "markup language"—a well-structured way of representing content on a web browser.

CSS

Cascading Style Sheets, or **CSS**, is supplementary code that visually enhances HTML. The introduction of CSS really spiced things up. It took the boring text, images, and layouts and gave them a makeover. It allowed for things such as nonvertical layouts of content, as well as more colors and great fonts. As a result, looking at a website was finally a pleasant experience, even though the viewer was still just looking at text and images.

JAVASCRIPT

Programming languages soon got thrown into the mix, and that was the start of something beautiful. Multiple programming languages jockeyed over which would be the definitive programming language for web browsers. JavaScript destroyed the competition. Embedding a programming language into a website's function was just the beginning.

JavaScript is, first and foremost, a programming language. But it includes a suite of Web-specific functionality that makes it easy to manipulate a website's content. Near the end of this book, there is an overview of how JavaScript works its magic on websites.

HTML is quite easy to learn. It is not as complex as JavaScript, but it is still outside the scope of this book. This book will provide HTML code snippets when needed. CSS, like HTML, won't be covered, but code will be provided. When presented in this book, the HTML and CSS code will be clearly indicated.

The Fundamentals

The hardest programming language to learn is the first one you pick up. The high-level concepts don't change across languages, and the way they interact with a computer is, for the most part, universal.

Big dreams start small. It's important to begin building your tool kit of programming knowledge with the fundamentals. So, let's take a look at some fundamental programming language that will be discussed within this book.

VARIABLES

Keeping track of data and huge lines of logic is a major challenge for a programmer, but there is a strategy to help you remember: **Variables**! Variables are used to associate names with data, and then refer back to them as needed. In practice, variables can be used for much more—but for now, all you need to know is that a variable is the concept of naming a piece of data so that it may be referred to later.

DATA TYPES

Multiple data types and data structures exist. A computer needs to know many different things before it starts doing all the heavy lifting for you. Are you trying to combine text or do math? Text and numbers are examples of data types. More advanced data types will be covered in this book, too.

DATA STRUCTURES

Data structures are containers for data. Data structures can hold one piece of data or millions of pieces. They are incredibly flexible and among the most powerful concepts in programming. Multiple types of data structures exist (such as arrays), and you will learn how to use the most basic ones.

CONDITIONAL STATEMENTS

To accommodate many situations in one particular set of code, it can have branching behavior: *"If this animal is a dog, then feed it chicken, but if this animal is a bird, feed it seeds."*

One statement handles two situations' possible outcomes. Using proper code can help make these kinds of decisions. In programming, the initial decision (that is, if the animal is a dog) is called a **conditional statement**.

LOOPS

Have you ever performed an activity that was repetitive and almost always the same each time? The computer version of that is called a **loop**. A loop is the process of automatically performing a set of operations repeatedly for as long as you tell it to.

Words to Know

As with any industry, programmers have their own lingo. Let's look at a few key words that will help you along the way.

ALGORITHM

An **algorithm** is a sequence of logical instructions that lead to a result or output.

Computers aren't the only things that use algorithms. Humans think in algorithms, too. Anything that is considered an "instruction" based on a set of rules is an algorithm. Algorithms come in all shapes, sizes, and difficulties. Humans are pretty flexible when it comes to instructions and have the unique power of critical thinking. This ability lets you fill in any incomplete or bad instructions using your past experiences.

But a computer has no critical thinking skills. It must be programmed. When computers receive instructions, they must be spoon-fed every detail. Even small deviations from your original intent could result in your algorithm stopping or doing something unexpected. These types of errors could have catastrophic consequences.

SYNTAX

All forms of written communication follow rules on how to structure words and statements. These rules are referred to as **syntax**. Some examples of syntax in the English language include:

→ End sentences with a period, exclamation point, or question mark.
→ Use "an" instead of "a" when the next word starts with a vowel.
→ Spell words correctly.
→ Use words according to their proper definition.

Programming languages have these types of rules, too. All programming languages have rigid structures that must be adhered to. But they take this demand for proper syntax to an extreme. Any single syntax rule violation will cause a program to break and fail to continue running. Thankfully, syntaxes for programming languages are easy to learn. The real challenge is to not make mistakes when writing it, or you'll have some debugging work ahead of you.

ABSTRACTION

Abstraction is the process of creating something that can perform a function or task, while hiding the details of how it does so. The concept of abstraction is not unique to code.

The world revolves around abstractions. Do you need to have a degree in electrical engineering in order to use a computer? Do you need to know how to assemble a car from scratch in order to get a driver's license? The abstraction mantra is: *"I don't need to know how it works. I only need to know how to use it."*

As your code grows in size, the need to hide unnecessary details from other parts of your code becomes important. There are multiple ways to create abstractions, and this book will equip you with the basic strategies.

PSEUDO CODE

There are two components to solving a programming challenge:

1. Have the correct way of thinking about the problem.
2. Implement the logic with no inconsistencies and no syntax errors.

Some problems are so challenging that a programmer does not want to solve both of those components at once. Instead, they figure out the correct way of thinking and write it down in plain English. This is referred to as **pseudo code**. After a programmer is confident that their line of reasoning will work, they implement it in real code. This book will use a lot of pseudo code. It'll help you when new concepts are introduced or when you are asked to solve challenging problems.

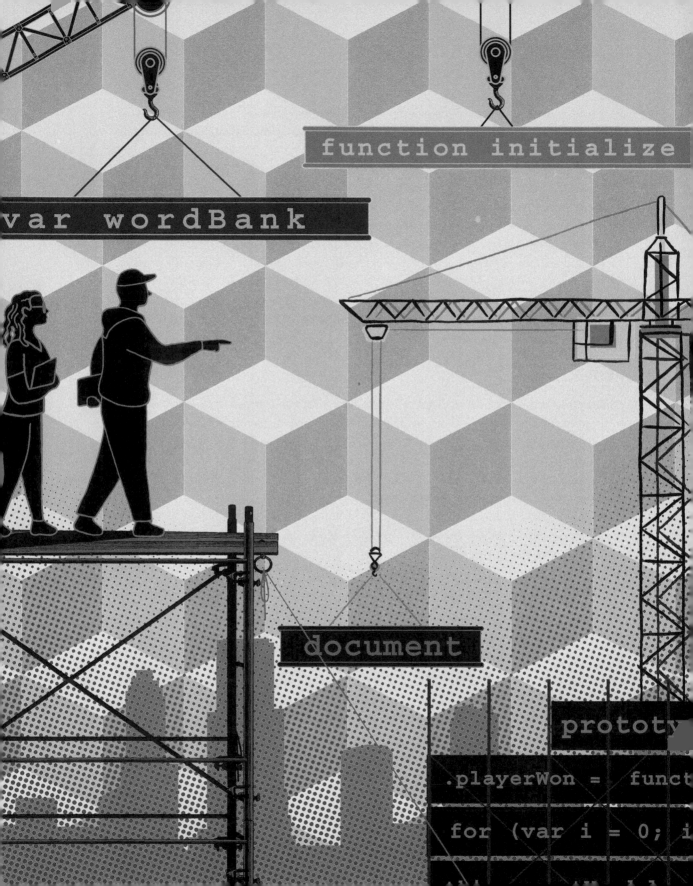

CHAPTER 2

JavaScript: Setting Up

Before starting on your exploration of JavaScript, you will need to set up your computer to run code. This chapter will provide step-by-step instructions for Windows and macOS computers. Make sure you get everything working before you continue to the next chapters. The rest of this book relies on it!

Coding Programs

You will use three different programs to code in JavaScript. Installation directions for each program will vary between PCs and Macs, so be sure to follow the directions for your operating system.

COMMAND LINE (GIT BASH FOR WINDOWS, TERMINAL FOR MACOS)

Programmers don't always work with nice point-and-click visual interfaces, such as your web browser. Oftentimes, you will need to type in text-based commands. It's nothing special. Just like running a program by pointing and clicking on an icon, you can type text-based instructions into a command line to perform operations.

TEXT EDITOR (VS CODE)

Programming is often very complex. Fortunately, very smart programmers have built incredible tools to help us be more productive, catch mistakes early, and read code easily. Programming text editors are programs that were designed completely around programming. They're kind of like Notepad, only better in every single way. They have smart features like autocomplete suggestions, color-code important text, autosave, and powerful shortcuts. We're going to use Visual Studio Code, or VS Code. It's one of the most popular free editors out there and has very good JavaScript support tools.

JAVASCRIPT RUNTIME (NODE.JS)

A command line is just a platform for performing computer operations. It does not have the ability to run JavaScript in its default state. We need to install another program, called Node.js, in order to run JavaScript code on our command line. We call the execution process of JavaScript code **runtime**.

DOWNLOADING METHODS

The most reliable way to find a website to download these programs is through a search engine. The best search terms are provided on pages 9 and 10. The most recent links (as of this writing) are also provided if you want to access the sites directly.

IMPORTANT DOWNLOAD INSTRUCTIONS

If the download is on a website and there are multiple file options, *do not* download anything that is labeled or has any of the following words in it: source code, Linux, Ubuntu, .deb, .tar.gz, .rar, and binary.

Those are for advanced users or users of other operating systems that we are not going to cover.

If you have the option for 32-bit or 64-bit, either one works. I always use 64-bit when it's available, since it's usually a little faster.

Windows (PC) Environment Setup

Always download an executable file labeled "windows", ".msi", or ".exe". If there are no labels anywhere in the download section and there is only one option, then download that. They will all be easy to install. Download and double-click to start the installation prompts.

You will need to install all three programs:

1. A good command line: **Git Bash**
2. Text editor: **VS Code**
3. JavaScript runtime: **Node.js**

GIT BASH

PCs come with a command line built in, but it can be difficult to work with. Instead, I suggest using a third-party application called Git Bash.

Search engine query: Git bash windows download

Current URL: **gitforwindows.org**

The installation process does not require any special configuration. While the insllation setup wizard runs, continue with all of the default configurations.

VS CODE

Search engine query: Visual studio code windows download
    Current URL: **code.visualstudio.com/download**
    When you download VS Code, click "Next" through all the prompts to install, but in the prompt "Select Additional Tasks," click on "Create a desktop icon to create an easily accessible shortcut on your desktop."

NODE.JS

Search engine query: Node js for windows download
    Current URL: **nodejs.org/en/download**
    Keep all of the default configurations during installation.
    Note: After finishing your Node.js installation, restart VS Code and any Git Bash windows you have open. This can be performed with the shortcut alt + F4. Alternatively, at the top right of the VS Code window, click the "x" icon to close it.

Mac Environment Setup

If a ".pkg" download is already available, use that one. It's the easiest installation method. Just double-click and it should automatically install. ".app" requires a drag-and-drop to the "Applications" folder. Double-click the ".app" file and a window should appear, asking you to drag and drop the file.

TERMINAL

Macs already come with a powerful and easy-to-use command line, called the "terminal." No Git Bash installation required.
    We will need to install only two applications:
1. Text editor: **VS Code**
2. JavaScript runtime: **Node.js**

VS CODE

Search engine query: Visual studio code windows download
    Current URL: **code.visualstudio.com/download**

NODE.JS

Search engine query: Node js mac download

    Current URL: **nodejs.org/en/download**

    Note: After finishing your Node.js installation, restart VS Code and any terminal windows you have open. Do this by typing command + q. Alternatively, at the top of your screen, you'll see a bar. Open "Code" and click "Quit Visual Studio Code." Save VS Code to your desktop so it's easy to find. This can be done by dragging it from your search bar onto your desktop.

Using a Code Editor

Knowing how to use a programming text editor effectively is an important skill. These programs have incredible depth of usability. But you don't need to learn too many features to gain plenty of value from them.

CODE EDITOR: AUTOFORMATTING

If you've seen computer code in the past, you may have noticed that there are indentations and spacings among lines. Nicely structured, right? Code is structured with white space and indentations for readability. This helps us follow the sequence of logic.

> ### Hacker Hint
>
> **If VS Code's color highlighting looks strange in certain places, there is a syntax error. If an autoformatted line spacing looks inconsistent, it likely means missing parentheses or curly brackets.**

CODE EDITOR: THE RED SQUIGGLES

It is important not to ignore the red squiggles under your code. VS Code, with its great JavaScript support, will do a basic analysis of your code and give you feedback on syntax errors. Those red squiggles indicate a fatal error in your code. JavaScript will not understand what you mean and will stop running your code. Not exactly ideal!

    If you see an error (marked by the red squiggles), hover your cursor over it and see what VS Code has to say about it. Sometimes, the error message won't be helpful. It might be jargon only experienced programmers will understand. But at the very least, it will tell you something's wrong.

Setting Up Your Terminal

VS Code has a feature that embeds your command line right into your text editor. To reveal it, go to View (at the top of your screen) -> Terminal.

Mac users don't need to do anything special, but Windows users will need to do a tiny bit of tweaking. The steps for doing so are included on the next few pages.

WINDOWS-ONLY INSTRUCTIONS FOR VS CODE TERMINAL

The default terminal that VS Code uses is the Windows built-in command line. As mentioned earlier, this command line is harder to work with, so we're going to use Git Bash as the default. After opening the terminal by going to Terminal (at the top of your screen) -> New Terminal, you will see, on the right-hand bar, a terminal selector. Click on "Select default shell."

A prompt will appear on the top. Select Git Bash.

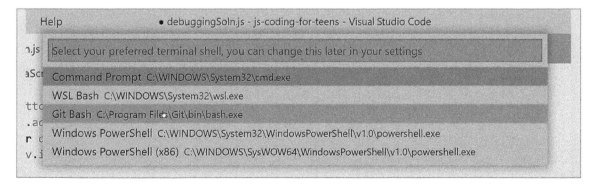

Restart VS Code. Look at the bottom of your screen. Your command line should now default to Git Bash when VS Code is opened.

PREPARE YOUR JAVASCRIPT FOLDER

It makes sense to have a folder in your computer that is dedicated to all of your code. Programmers call this a "working directory." Create a folder anywhere in your file system, preferably somewhere easily accessible, like your desktop folder. All of the files that contain your code will live in this folder.

To open the folder, click "File" then "Open Folder" in VS Code.

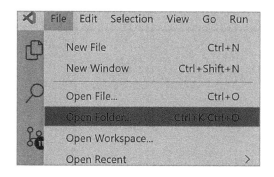

Find the folder you created and click "Select Folder."

Once you open it, VS Code should now have the name of the folder on the top bar.

INSTALLING JAVASCRIPT PACKAGES

Many algorithms are hard to write, so programmers all over the world share their code with one another so they don't have to reinvent difficult algorithms all over again! They are uploaded to a hosting service called **npm** (short for "Node Package Manager"), which is available to everyone to download for free. Installing packages is a streamlined process for a user. In JavaScript, creating basic programs with user interactivity is surprisingly complicated. In many of the exercises within this book, you will be using a handy package someone else worked very hard to make, named **readline-sync**. The command to install it through the terminal is:

```
npm i readline-sync
```

But wait—where do you type this? Easy enough: In the bottom half of your screen, beneath the word "terminal," is the terminal. In that area, you'll probably see a small white box. This is where you'll type your terminal commands. If you don't see something similar to the image below at the bottom of your window, you haven't opened the VS Code terminal. This can be done on the menu bar at Terminal -> New Terminal.

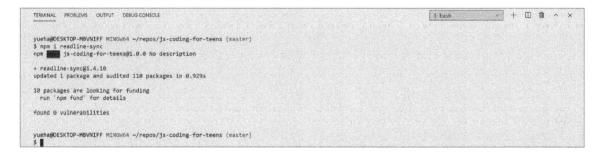

PREPARE THE FILE

Go to File -> New File and it will open up a new, empty text file for you to start coding in. To save a file, go to File -> Save. Let's try this out. When you first save a file, it will ask you to name it. The default extension will be for a .txt file. But don't save yet, because it's a trap!

You're using JavaScript. You have to give it the JavaScript file extension, which is .js. As long as you have the correct file extension, .js, it can be named anything. But I suggest "index.js."

DOUBLE-CHECKING

Make sure you have your folder open in VS Code. VS Code's terminal will automatically point to your folder's directory. The easiest way to find and run your code in the terminal is to have it already pointing to the directory your files live in. To double-check, type in the command `ls` (FYI, that's a lowercase L). It will print out all of the files and folders in the current directory. You should see your file, index.js, in the terminal output.

Writing Your First Code

Now you're properly equipped to run some JavaScript! But before you can run any code, you have to write it.

CONSOLE.LOG

We'll be constantly using something called **console.log**. **console.log** takes what is wrapped in its parentheses and prints it onto the command line. At this point, you don't need to understand the underlying mechanisms behind **console.log**. We're just here to confirm that your computer is ready to write JavaScript!

LET'S WRITE SOME JAVASCRIPT!

We'll keep it simple for now, with a single **console.log**. Type this into your file in VS Code, but don't hit Enter. Save the file as a .js file after you're done.

```
console.log('salutations terra!');
```

LET'S RUN SOME JAVASCRIPT!

The syntax to run commands on a command line is always as follows:

```
[command] [parameters]
```

Node.js is your runtime. The command is **node**, and the parameter is the file name.

```
node index.js
```

Congrats! You have officially run your first piece of code.

Bugs

Writing an algorithm is like writing a persuasive essay. An algorithm is a body of writing in which the logic flow leads to the correct conclusion. You get graded on the following criteria:

1. Answered: Your essay comes to the correct conclusion.
2. Grammar: No written language rules are broken.
3. Good justification: Your reasoning throughout the essay makes sense.

Writing code has similar requirements:

1. Answered: You have expected behavior.
2. Grammar: Correct JavaScript syntax.
3. Good justification: Your algorithm's sequence of logic is bulletproof.

Teachers tend to be kind, or at least mildly flexible, when it comes to grades. A computer is ruthless. Here is how a computer grades your code.

1. Not expected behavior? Partial credit, but still a failing score.
2. Incorrect syntax? Runtime error. 0/100
3. One mistake in algorithm? Runtime error. 0/100

You need a perfect score when writing code. Any deviation means you have one or more imperfections in your code. We refer to imperfections as **bugs**. If you want that passing score, you'll need to find them all.

Professional programmers create programs with an unbelievable amount of code. They are referred to as **codebases**. Bugs love to hide in nooks and crannies of thousands (if not millions) of lines of code. It's a tough job, but programmers strive to write bug-free code.

> **Hacker Hint**
>
> **Feeling burnt out? Take a 15-minute break. You will come back with a clearer head and find the bug sooner than you think.**

BUGS CAN BE FRUSTRATING

When you begin coding, you will write a lot of imperfect code. You will get it wrong the first time, the second time, maybe even the twentieth time. But the most important part about bugs is to not let them get to your head. Even professional programmers get frustrated. It is all part of the learning process, so don't give up!

CHAPTER 3

Variables and Data Types

In order to code effectively, it is important to understand the fundamental tool kit JavaScript gives you. In this chapter, you'll be learning about the various types of data used to represent concepts when writing code. You'll also learn the strategies programmers use to keep track of this data. The way programmers structure their code is also very important. It's what gives us the ability to effectively read one another's code.

Code Structure

Programming languages have baseline rules about how they should be written. Let's go over them before you get your hands dirty. This is just a high-level overview to understand how JavaScript code is structured. No need to think about the content of the lines.

STATEMENTS

A **statement** is an expression that performs an action. Statements are usually written on a single line.

```
console.log('I am a statement');
var statement = 'I am another statement';
```

SEMICOLONS

Have you noticed the semicolons? Each statement should have a semicolon at the end. JavaScript has some sneaky ways of fixing itself if you forget, but it's finicky and prone to errors. Play it safe and get into the habit of always adding the semicolon yourself.

There are situations where semicolons at the end of a statement are illegal syntax. I'll explain those situations as we go along.

COMMENTS

There are times when a programmer wants to write text that should not be run, like a note to yourself. A **comment** is a way of writing information in the file that will be ignored when the code is run.

You can write whatever you want, for whatever reason. Complex algorithms can get hairy, and comments are one way to help explain what the code is doing. The syntax is adding double slashes in front of the text that is not code.

```
// outputs text to the browser console or terminal
console.log('I am a statement');
```

INDENTATIONS

You will notice indentations on some lines. It is intentional, but technically optional. Programmers indent code for readability. Any coding text editor will guide you toward proper indentation. As you write more code, you will begin to understand the rules.

Variables

Robots have not taken over the world yet, so I assume that you, the reader, are human. For humans, the concept of a name is a system for creating a unique identity. In the same way you and I have different names to keep track of each other, names in programming are used to identify and keep track of data. Coding names are referred to as **variables**.

DECLARATION

Associating data with a variable is a two-step process. The first step is to **declare** a variable. The process of declaration is telling JavaScript that a particular name should be prepared as a variable. The special word **var** tells JavaScript that a variable should be declared.

```
// declaration
var aHumanName;
```

ASSIGNMENT

The association of data with a variable is **assignment**. Once a variable has been declared, it does not need to be redeclared. Assignment is executed with the equal sign operator.

```
// declaration
var aHumanName;
// assignment
aHumanName = 'Andrew';
```

ASSIGNMENT AND DECLARATION IN ONE STATEMENT

Declaration and assignment are two distinct ideas, but they are often performed in one statement.

```
// declaration and assignment in one statement
var aHumanName = 'Andrew';
```

DATA REASSIGNMENT

Variables can also be **reassigned** to different values. The ability to reassign is important for upcoming topics.

```
// declaration and assignment
var aHumanName = 'Andrew';
// assign variable to a new value
aHumanName = 'Charlie';
```

EVALUATING STATEMENTS WITH VARIABLES

Every time a variable is used, JavaScript will extract the data the variable is associated with and use it in its place.

```
var myBirthYear = 1990;
var currentYear = 2021;
// equivalent of 2021 - 1990
currentYear - myBirthYear;
```

KEYWORDS CAN'T BE VARIABLES

The word **var** is one example of a **keyword** in JavaScript. Its usage always means "a variable declaration." It will ignore any other intent and is off-limits for variable names.

```
// will create runtime error! variable declaration expected
var var = 2021;
```

The code you've just witnessed here is a request to declare a declaration of nothing and assigning nothing to the number 2021. Confused? So is JavaScript.

VARIABLE NAME CONVENTION

Programmers like to keep the structure of variables consistent. This is commonly referred to as **convention**. JavaScript convention for variable names is **camelCase**: Lowercase for the first word, with all subsequent words capitalized—get the reference to the hump in the middle?

```javascript
// accepted camelCase convention
var currentYear = 2021;
// will not break in runtime but it would be better if you did not
var current_year = 2021;
// we are no longer friends
var xXx_CuRrEnTyEaR_xXx = 2021;
```

Later on, we will use different conventions for specific topics. For now, always use camelCase.

Data Types

Now that you know how variables work, it is time to learn about the types of data that can be assigned to them.

NUMBER

Numbers follow basic arithmetic rules. Order of operations is: parentheses, exponents, multiplication, division, addition, and then subtraction.

```javascript
10 + 20; // 30
20 * 10; // 200
(20 + 3) * 10; // 230 - respects order of operations
```

INCREMENT OPERATOR

In programming, increasing or decreasing the value of a variable by 1 is a common operation, so there is a shorthand for it. Use double-plus and double-minus operators to **increment** and **decrement**, respectively.

```
var num = 1;
num++; // num is now 2
num--; // num is now back to 1
```

Never Assign an Increment Statement

Be careful not to assign when incrementing, because the value of the variable won't change if you do. Unexpected behavior will occur.

```
var num = 1;
num++; // good!
num = num++; // no! bad!
```

SELF-OPERATING MATH SHORTHAND

Performing math on a variable and then reassigning the previous value is another common thing to do. Programmers have a shorthand for it. An umbrella term for these operators is **arithmetic assignment**. It is a math operator and assign operator joined into a single operator.

```
var num = 1;
num += 2; // same as num = num + 2
num; // 3
var num = 1;
num *= 3; // works the same way for multiplication and division
num; // 3
```

NAN: NOT A NUMBER

Numbers seem easy, right? Well, it's time to talk about the dark side of numbers.

There is a special number type that is not a number. Yes, you read that correctly. It's a number that represents something that is not a number. Its name is **NaN**, which stands for "Not a Number."

NaN is a keyword that is a numeric value. Math can be performed on it. Any math attempted on **NaN** will compute to **NaN**.

```
NaN * 10; // NaN
```

How does one get **NaN** to begin with? In order to do so, you have to do something mathematically illogical.

```
10 / 'dog'; // NaN
```

What is "10 divided by dog"? JavaScript considers this nonsense to be NaN.

Strings

A collection of characters is referred to as a **string**. Think of it as a "string of characters." Creating a string is simple. You simply have to wrap text in quotes. Double and single quotes both work to develop strings.

```
// both valid strings
"dog";
'dog';
```

STRING CONCATENATION

JavaScript has a lot of clever tricks up its sleeve when it comes to modifying strings. But for now, the only thing you need to know is that strings can be combined with the addition operator. The concept of combining strings is called **concatenation**, or **concat** for short. Any number of strings can be combined using the plus operator.

```
'one ' + 'two'; // 'one two'
'one ' + 'two' + 'three' + 'four'; // 'one two three four'
```

Notice the empty space at the end of all the strings except the last one? That's because spaces are characters, too. They are needed to separate words when performing concatenation.

SELF-OPERATING STRING CONCATENATION SHORTHAND

In the same way that math is commonly computed and reassigned to the same variable, strings are concatenated and reassigned as well. Technically, a string is also called the **addition assignment**. The addition assignment operator can be used for both.

```
var numWords = 'one two'; // 'one two'
numWords += 'three four';
numWords; // 'one two three four'
```

ESCAPE CHARACTERS

Wrapping text in quotes indicates a string. But what if you want a quote inside a string?

```
'hello, my dog's name is Suzy'; // runtime error
```

JavaScript is reading this as a string that stops at **dog**. The apostrophe in **"dog's"** throws it off. The subsequent text is interpreted as nonsense code and will break in runtime. In order to express that the apostrophe in **"dog's"** should be part of the string, we need to **escape** it. This is accomplished using the backslash operator.

```
'hello, my dog\'s name is Suzy'; // much better
```

NUMBERS AND STRINGS: THE DIFFERENCE

A string is considered text. In that sense, we can have a string that looks like a number, but actually is not. The number ten (**10**) and a string comprising a "1" and a "0" (**"10"**) are interpreted differently. Numbers can have math operated on them. But the concept of mathematical operations on text does not make real-world sense, right?

```
10; // the number ten
'10'; // text with two characters: 1 and 0
```

Boolean

Simply put, a **boolean** is a data type that is either the keyword **true** or **false**. Their respective keywords mean exactly what you think.

```
// boolean keywords
true;
false;
```

Data checking is the most common way to attain a boolean value. We'll do lots of data checking when we learn about **conditionals**. For now, just know that the keywords **true** and **false** exist.

null

Sometimes you want to express the idea of "nothing." This is where the keyword **null** comes into play. It literally means "nothing."

```
// keyword null
null;
```

undefined

Another keyword that loosely represents nothing is **undefined**. More specifically, it represents "something that has not been assigned a value."

```
// keyword undefined
undefined;
```

So far, the only way we have discussed how to get the value **undefined** is by declaring a variable but not assigning it a value.

```
var aName; // undefined
```

Type Coercion

Dear reader, I'm so sorry, but I cannot live this lie anymore. You can, in fact, perform math with mixes of numbers and strings—sometimes.

```
// the number 30 minus the string '20' equals the number 10
30 - '20'; // 10
```

After JavaScript sees an operation that doesn't make sense, like math with a number and a string, sometimes it will try to do something called **type coercion.** It is the concept of performing operations on two fundamentally different data types that result in an actual output.

CONFUSING TYPE COERCION

Some may consider this a strong opinion, but I find type coercion to be the embodiment of the saying "Just because you can doesn't mean you should."

Many of the rules behind type coercion, to be blunt, are absolutely ridiculous. Let's look at an example of what I mean. Below is a noncomprehensive list of examples that will melt your brain if you try and write thousands of lines of code heavily reliant on type coercion.

```
// the number 30 minus the string '20' equals the number 10
30 - '20'; // 10
// if it is addition, string concatenation takes priority over addition
30 + '20'; // '3020'
// null coerces to 0
10 + null; // 10
```

One of the very few exceptions is the conversion of a number to a string by using the concat operator on an empty string.

```
// conversion to a number -> string using type coercion
'' + 10; // '10'
```

If all of that completely confused you, that's kind of the point—type coercion is not something to rely on. It is, at best, slightly helpful. At its worst, it will leave you scratching your head at code that runs but creates the wrong output.

Data Structures

In real-world scenarios, programmers operate on vast amounts of data. Many modern programs deal with thousands, if not millions, of pieces of data.

Because of this, it makes perfect sense for programmers to create data management strategies. Instead of assigning individual pieces of data to a variable, one by one, why not make something that is a collection of many pieces of data? This is what a **data structure** is.

JavaScript provides two basic data structures to manage data. They are called **arrays** and **objects**.

Objects

Objects are data structures. They hold their data in **key-value pairs**. Keys are also referred to as **properties** of the object.

```javascript
var dogBreedAndName = {
    terrier: 'suzy', // key: terrier, value: 'suzy'
    shiba: 'yin-yin', // key: shiba, value: 'yin-yin'
    goldenRetriever: 'sparky' // key: goldenRetriever, value: 'sparky'
};
```

Accessing values is done by referring to the associated key name. This can be performed with the **dot operator** (a period).

```javascript
// get the value 'suzy' by accessing the key 'terrier'
dogBreedAndName.terrier; // 'suzy'
```

Bracket notation also works. It accesses the value using the string value of the key.

```javascript
// get the value 'suzy' by accessing the key 'terrier'
dogBreedAndName['terrier']; // 'suzy'
```

OBJECTS AND UNDEFINED

Any attempt to access a key that does not exist will output **undefined**.

```javascript
var dogs = {
    terrier: 'suzy'
};
// No key 'shiba' exists in the object
dogs.shiba; // undefined.
```

DOT OPERATOR VS. BRACKET NOTATION

The **dot operator** cannot access anything except the name that has been explicitly declared. The following will not work.

```
var dogName = 'terrier';
dogBreedAndName.dogName; // undefined
```

The intention of this code is to use **"terrier"** as a key to access the string **"suzy"**. But in this case, the variable **dogName** was assigned first. The dot operator will attempt to access the name as a string.

```
// equivalent statements
dogBreedAndName.dogName; // undefined
dogBreedAndName['dogName']; // undefined
```

Accessing values from a variable name must use bracket notation.

```
var dogName = 'terrier';
dogBreedAndName[dogName]; // 'suzy'
```

Arrays

An **array** is a data structure with a syntax of square brackets, with commas separating each piece of data from the other.

```
[1, 2, 3]; // an array of numbers
```

Arrays have **indexes**. Indexes are "slots" that can have data inserted into them. Each item inside an array can be accessed by index using bracket notation. Indexes in an array start at 0.

```
var array = [30, 21, 43, 34];
array[0]; // 30
array[1]; // 21
array[2]; // 43
array[3]; // 34
```

ARRAYS AND UNDEFINED

An attempt to access an index that is out of the bounds of the size of the array will cause problems in your code. Your output will be **undefined**.

```
var array = [30, 21, 43, 34];
// array is not long enough to have an index of 4
array[4]; // undefined
```

ARRAY PROPERTY: LENGTH

More will be explained later in this book, but arrays also have the concept of **properties**. The most important one that will be used is the **length** property.

```
var array = [30, 21, 43, 34];
array.length; // 4
```

Data and Variables in Action

Let's imagine you have lots of dogs and want the option to provide the dog breed and print out the name of each of your dogs. Let's take everything you've learned so far and apply it!

RECAP: CONFIRM FILE LOCATION

For your first challenge, let's re-review the file-creation and code-running processes. Create a file and name it **dogNames.js**. Here is what my VS Code explorer looks like right now. Yours may look different. You can manage your files however you'd like.

HACKER HINT

If you've gone into the wrong nested directory, the command to go back up is cd .. (the command cd, a space, and two periods). If you're completely lost, restarting VS Code will reset the directory.

RECAP: CONFIRM LOCATION IN TERMINAL

Remember your terminal command `ls`? Use it to confirm that the command line is currently pointed to the right folder.

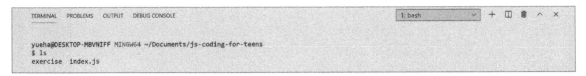

Uh-oh! You're in the wrong directory. Your **dogNames.js** file isn't there. After inspecting your explorer, you see that it is nested in two subfolders: "exercises" and "ch3." You need to point to the right directory or you can't run your code. You can do it using the terminal command **cd**.

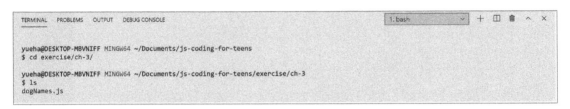

Double-check with `ls` to confirm the correct location.

PREPPING INTERACTIVITY

Add your first snippet of JavaScript to prepare for the exercise.

```
// the content of our file
var prompt = require('readline-sync');
var breed = prompt.question('what breed is your dog? ');
```

Don't sweat the details. Just know that these two lines make the JavaScript interactable. Running this code will create a text prompt. After entering text, it will be saved to the variable **breed**.

Taking things one step at a time helps you find bugs sooner. Before trying to solve any challenges, print the input variable **breed**.

The file should temporarily look like this. Remember to save the file before running it.

```
// the content of our file
var prompt = require('readline-sync');
var breed = prompt.question('what breed is your dog? ');
console.log(breed);
```

RUN THE CODE

An interactive experience has been prepared! Use the terminal command **node** and the file name to run it.

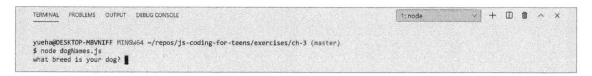

Good! Now your JavaScript is waiting for you to type in a dog breed. Type something in and press Enter.

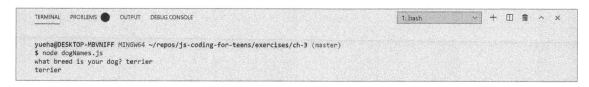

You have now confirmed that your code is accepting user inputs and printing out values in your command line.

ADD DATA

With a prompt set up, create a data structure with lovely dog information. Any key-value pairs can be added. As an example, I will provide excellent names that any dog would enjoy being called.

```javascript
var dogs = {
    terrier: 'Suzy',
    husky: 'Sir Sniffybums III',
    pug: 'Notorious P.U.G.'
};
```

PRINT AN INTERESTING STRING

You now have input capability and data. Perhaps it is time for you to print an interesting string? To do this, you are going to use string concatenation, a string escape character, and data access of an object using bracket notation in one line.

```
console.log('Your dog\'s name is ' + dogs[breed] + '? How fascinating!');
```
The file should now look like this.

```
// dogNames.js
var prompt = require('readline-sync');
var breed = prompt.question('what breed is your dog? ');
var dogs = {
    terrier: 'Suzy',
    husky: 'Sir Sniffybums III',
    pug: 'Notorious P.U.G.'
};
console.log('Your dog\'s name is ' + dogs[breed] + '? How fascinating!');
```

RUN THE FILE AGAIN

Remember to save. Run the code one more time.

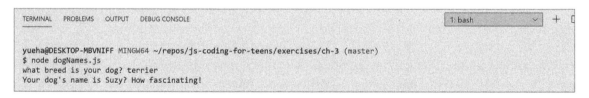

```
TERMINAL   PROBLEMS   OUTPUT   DEBUG CONSOLE                          1: bash         ∨   +  

yueha@DESKTOP-MBVNIFF MINGW64 ~/repos/js-coding-for-teens/exercises/ch-3 (master)
$ node dogNames.js
what breed is your dog? terrier
Your dog's name is Suzy? How fascinating!
```

With the input **terrier**, the object accessed the **terrier** key and gave the string value "**Suzy**". But what if we type a string that is not a key in our object?

```
TERMINAL   PROBLEMS   OUTPUT   DEBUG CONSOLE                          1: bash         ∨

yueha@DESKTOP-MBVNIFF MINGW64 ~/repos/js-coding-for-teens/exercises/ch-3 (master)
$ node dogNames.js
what breed is your dog? shiba
Your dog's name is undefined? How fascinating!
```

We can agree to disagree, but I find **undefined** to be a terrible name for a dog. Clearly, this is an oversight in the code. It would be nice if you could communicate this. However, at this point, you don't have the knowledge to address this. This is something to look forward to in the next chapter.

Crack the Code

1. When are comments useful?
2. What is the difference between declaration and assignment?
3. Can the word **var** be used as a variable name? Why or why not?
4. What keywords were covered in this chapter?
5. What is the main difference between increment operators and self-assignment operators?
6. How are values in an array accessed?
7. How are values in an object accessed?
8. What value is outputted if a nonexistent index is accessed in an array?
9. What value is outputted if a nonexistent key is accessed in an object?
10. When is bracket notation necessary for accessing a value in an object, instead of the dot operator?

Debugging

When debugging code, it can be helpful to place the code in a file and run it in the command line. You will get real-time feedback on your answer.

1. The variable doesn't seem to change in value, despite the fact that it is being incremented.

```
var num = 0;
num = num++; // increment num
console.log(num); // 0
```

2. Adding two numbers together isn't working properly.

```
var num1 = 10;
var num2 = '2';
console.log(num1 + num2); // '102'
```

3. Trying to access your dog's name **"Max"** by using the key **"pug"** is outputting **undefined**.

```
var dogs = {
    pug: 'Max',
    terrier: 'Appa'
};
```

```
var myDog = 'pug';
console.log(dogs.myDog); // undefined
```

4. An attempt to access the last entry in the array is outputting **undefined**.
```
var meanPeople = ['Layna', 'Layna again', 'Layna one more time'];
console.log(meanPeople[3]); // undefined
```

5. A fatal runtime error is occurring when trying to print this string.
```
console.log('Layna's favorite hobby is being mean
to Andrew'); // Uncaught SyntaxError: missing ) after argument list
```

CODER'S CHECKLIST » Let's review the topics we covered

Let's take a quick minute to review what was covered in this chapter. An understanding of arrays and data types are especially important.

- Data types
- Type coercion
- Data structures— arrays and objects
- Accessing data within data structures

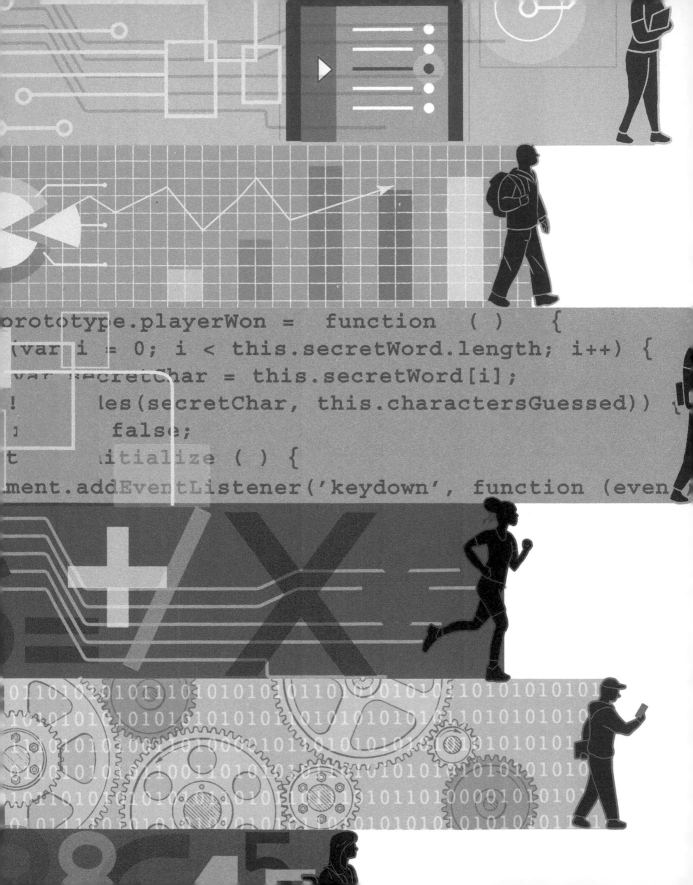

```
rototype.playerWon =  function  ( )   {
(var i = 0; i < this.secretWord.length; i++) {
var secretChar = this.secretWord[i];
!    les(secretChar, this.charactersGuessed))
1      false;
t      itialize ( ) {
ment.addEventListener('keydown', function (even
```

CHAPTER 4

Conditionals

Computers operate in very logical ways. Some of a computer's favorite answers are "yes" and "no." In computer terms, this is the equivalent of "true" and "false." The ability to discern between true and false is an incredible strength. It means a computer can decide what code should run depending on the situation. This also means that one program can do many things and make its own decisions! The decisions are controlled using **conditionals**.

Data Checking and Validation

Before leveraging the power of conditionals, the strategies that are used to create proper decision-making need to be covered. The raw values **true** and **false** are not commonly used in conditionals. Instead, they are almost always computed through other operations.

Equality Operators

The most common comparison operation that will be made is checking if two values are identical or not identical.

EQUALITY OPERATOR

The **equality operator**, denoted as a double equal sign, checks if two values are identical.

```
10 == 10; // true
'pizza' == 'pizza'; // true
'pizza' == 'Pizza'; // false
false == false; // true
```

Ready for an unfun surprise? The equality operator will use **type coercion** if possible.

```
'10' == 10; // true
```

It is recommended to not use the equality operator. A different operator does a better job for the same purpose.

STRICT EQUALITY OPERATOR

The **strict equality operator** is the equality operator's more logical sibling, denoted as a triple equal sign. It checks equality and never uses type coercion.

```
10 === 10; // true
'pizza' === 'pizza'; // true
'pizza' === 'Pizza'; // false
false === false; // true
// no type coercion performed
'10' === 10; // false
```

INEQUALITY OPERATOR

The **inequality operator**, denoted as an exclamation point and equal sign, checks if two values are not identical.

```
10 != 10; // false
'pizza' != 'pizza'; // false
'pizza' != 'Pizza'; // true
false != false; // false
```

Just like with the equality operator, the inequality operator will use type coercion.

```
'10' != 10; // false
```

STRICT INEQUALITY OPERATOR

The **strict inequality operator** is the better version of the inequality operator. Just like strict equality, strict inequality does not perform any type coercion. Compared to regular inequality, it is the safer bet for JavaScript code. Its syntax is denoted as an exclamation point and double equal sign. Please use this instead of the regular inequality operator.

```
10 !== 10; // false
'pizza' !== 'pizza'; // false
'pizza' !== 'Pizza'; // true
false !== false; // false
// no type coercion performed
'10' !== 10; // true
```

Relational Operators

In the same way two values can be checked for equality or inequality, values can be checked for whether they are greater than or less than.

LESS THAN OPERATORS

Two available comparison operators are the **less than operator** and the **less than or equal to operator**. They do exactly what they sound like. Numbers are compared numerically, and strings are compared alphabetically. It is important to note that capitalization matters,

```
10 < 8; // false
'a' < 'b'; // true
'A' > 'a'; // false
10 <= 8; // false
```

GREATER THAN OPERATORS

The **greater than operator** and **greater than or equal to operator** share the same principles as the less than operators, and capitalization still matters.

```
10 > 8; // true
'a' > 'b'; // false
'a' >= 'b'; // true
```

Logical Operators

Aside from basic equality operators, JavaScript provides special operators that help create boolean values in complex situations. Many **logical operators** and equality operators can be mixed and matched.

OR OPERATOR

The **OR operator**, denoted as double pipes, checks to see if either operation is true.

```
true || false; // true
false || false; // false
false || true || false; // true
```

AND OPERATOR

The **AND operator**, denoted as a double ampersand, checks to see if both operations output to true.

```
true && true; // true
true && false; // false
false && false; // false
false && true && false; // false
```

NOT OPERATOR

In programming, there is also the concept of a **NOT operator**, denoted as an exclamation point in front of a value. This operator is commonly referred to as the **bang operator**. It flips the boolean value of the value it is operated on.

```
!true; // false
!false; // true
```

Mix and Match Logical Operators and Equalities

The keywords **true** and **false** are rarely used in code. Now that you have equality comparator operators and logical operators in your tool kit, you will see conditions that range from simple to complex in code.

```
// 1 is greater than 10 OR 1 is equal to 0
1 > 10 || 1 === 0; // false
// 1 is less than 10 OR 1 is equal to 0
1 < 10 || 1 === 0; // true
```

Data Validation

Checking if a value is **undefined** or **null** is easy.

```
var mySocialLife = null;
mySocialLife === null; // true
```

The equality operator handles it, because those data types have one possible value. But what about numbers, strings, booleans, and arrays? What if you aren't interested in the value of the number? Perhaps you simply want to know whether or not it is a number. Luckily, there are operators for these situations.

TYPEOF OPERATOR

The **typeof** operator outputs the variable's data type, in the form of a string. This is especially helpful when debugging code. Incorrect data types are a common source of errors!

```
typeof 10; // 'number'
typeof ''; // 'string'
typeof undefined; // 'undefined'
typeof true; // 'boolean'
```

Simple stuff. But let me throw a curveball at you.

```
typeof null; // 'object'–what????
```

Huh? Why doesn't **typeof null** output the string **null**? It is debatable as to whether this is a bug. But at the end of the day, it is incredibly unintuitive. Instead, check for **null** using the equality operator.

```
null === null // true
```

INSTANCEOF OPERATOR

When checking whether an item is an array, the **typeof** operator is very deceptive.

```
typeof []; // 'object'
```

The underlying reason why the output is **"object"** technically makes sense, but it is unhelpful and unintuitive. Array validation can be properly performed using the **instanceof** operator.

```
[] instanceof Array; // true
```

Note that **Array** is not a string in this situation. This is contrasting **typeof**, which outputs a string.

Don't Use instanceof for Objects

Checking to see if a value is an object is extremely challenging. That's because **typeof** and **instanceof** don't work. The worst part is that they appear to work, but this is not the case.

```
var anObject = {};
anObject instanceof Object; // true
typeof anObject === 'object'; // true
```

The problem lies in the fact that too many nonobject values will output the exact same thing when **typeof** and **instanceof** are called on them.

```
[] instanceof Object; // true
typeof [] === 'object'; // true
```

Conditional Statements

After learning about all of the ways to validate data and compare values, you are ready to use them to solve meaningful challenges. The most common conditional statements are **if . . . else if . . . else** statements.

Conditional Branching Statements

The term "conditional branching statements" is a fancy way of describing an **if . . . else if . . . else** statement. It allows a programmer to perform actions based on certain conditions.

IF STATEMENT

An **if statement** runs code if the condition evaluates to true. The keyword is **if**, with parentheses around the condition and curly brackets wrapping the operations. Any number of operations can be placed inside an if statement. Notice that there are no semicolons.

```
if (condition) {
    // do something here
}
```
Let's conditionally modify a string, based on its value.
```
var dogName = 'Max';
if (dogName === 'Max') {
    dogName += ' is an awesome dog';
}
dogName; // 'Max is an awesome dog'
```
Great! We love dogs named Max.

ELSE STATEMENT

What if you want to express your disdain for dogs that are not named Max? That is where the **else statement** comes into play. After an **if** statement, an **else** statement can be chained to it. If the **if** condition fails, the **else** statement's code will run.

```
var dogName = 'Layna';
if (dogName === 'Max') {
    dogName += ' is an awesome dog';
} else {
    dogName += ' is NOT an awesome dog';
}
dogName; // 'Layna is NOT an awesome dog'
```

A dog that is named Layna? Inconceivable.

ELSE IF STATEMENT

What if you also decide that Charlie is an acceptable name for a dog? An **else if statement** can be added to the conditional chain. It follows the same syntax as an `if` statement.

```
var dogName = 'Charlie';
if (dogName === 'Max') {
    dogName += ' is an awesome dog';
} else if (dogName === 'Charlie') {
    dogName += ' is an okay dog';
} else {
    dogName += ' is NOT an awesome dog';
}
dogName; // 'Charlie is an okay dog'
```

Conditionals in Action

Remember our challenge from the previous chapter?

```
var prompt = require('readline-sync');
var breed = prompt.question('what breed is your dog? ');
var dogs = {
    terrier: 'Suzy',
    husky: 'Sir Sniffybums III',
    pug: 'Notorious P.U.G.'
};
console.log('Your dog\'s name is ' + dogs[breed] + '? How fascinating!');
```

```
TERMINAL    PROBLEMS    OUTPUT    DEBUG CONSOLE                                    1: bash          ∨

yueha@DESKTOP-MBVNIFF MINGW64 ~/repos/js-coding-for-teens/exercises/ch-3 (master)
$ node dogNames.js
what breed is your dog? shiba
Your dog's name is undefined? How fascinating!
```

When the **breed** does not exist in the object, the output was **undefined**. That's not a good representation of what is happening, because the real issue is that the **dogs** object does not account for every breed on the planet. The code should communicate this.

Using conditionals, let's solve our previous problem! Before implementing this, let's write some pseudo code.

CONDITIONALS HAVE MULTIPLE APPROACHES

For algorithms that involve conditionals, there are many ways to say the same thing. Here are two different ways to say the same thing:

```
If we find the breed in the object then print: our dog name. Else, print:
dog not found
If we do not find a breed, then print: dog not found. Else, print: our
dog name
```

When you think about it, these are two sides of the same coin. They say the exact same thing, except in opposite order. Let's express your two possible statements using JavaScript syntax.

```
if (we find a value) {
    print our dog name
} else {
    print dog not found
}
if (we do not find a value) {
    print dog not found
} else {
    print our dog name
}
```

Translating this logic requires you to think like a computer. You need the JavaScript equivalent of "find a value." Accessing a key in an object that does not exist, you get

undefined. If the value is **undefined**, that implies that the key does not exist. There are two different ways of writing this.

```
typeof value === 'undefined';
value === undefined;
```

Same difference, right? Let's use the second one. Finally, your code from chapter 3 makes sense!

```
var prompt = require('readline-sync');
var breed = prompt.question('what breed is your dog? ');
var dogs = {
    terrier: 'Suzy',
    husky: 'Sir Sniffybums III',
    pug: 'Notorious P.U.G.'
};
if (dogs[breed] === undefined) {
    console.log('A dog was not found :(');
} else {
    console.log('Your dog\'s name is ' + dogs[breed] + '? How
fascinating!');
}
```

```
TERMINAL    PROBLEMS    OUTPUT    DEBUG CONSOLE                                    1: bash            ⌄

yueha@DESKTOP-MBVNIFF MINGW64 ~/repos/js-coding-for-teens/exercises/ch-3 (master)
$ node dogNames.js
what breed is your dog? greyhound
A dog was not found :(
```

Much better. There are no dogs named **undefined**. The output is now properly communicating what is happening within the code.

Crack the Code

Some very important concepts have been introduced in this chapter. Before continuing further, make sure you have full confidence in your answers to the following questions. This is important, because moving forward, conditionals will be used extensively.

1. What is the difference between equality operators and strict equality operators?
2. What data types can the **typeof** operator properly check?
3. What data type uses the **instanceof** operator for proper checking?
4. What is the output of the following code?

```
(true && false) || false;
```

5. What is the output of the following code?

```
!false || (false && true);
```

6. Why is `array[index] !== undefined` an effective way of checking to see if that index exists inside an array?

Debugging

Ready for a few challenges? Remember to run the code in your terminal to actively see what is happening!

1. The code is saying that **item** is not an array.

```
var item = [];
if (typeof item === 'array') {
    console.log('I am an array');
} else {
    console.log('I am not an array');
}
// I am not an array
```

2. Dr. Donkey is a professional game critic and has reviewed many games. Here are a few of them, along with their respective scores.

```
var donkeysGameScores = {
    superItalianBrosTwo: 100,
    theLastDefender: 40,
    leagueOfHeroes: 30,
    aldaAndTheFluteOfTime: 98
};
```

Super Italian Bros Two has won Dr. Donkey's "Game of the Year" award more than 10 times in a row. It definitely is a masterpiece. But the code is saying otherwise.

```
var game = 'superItalianBrosTwo';
if (donkeysGameScores[game] < 95) {
    console.log(game + ' is a masterpiece');
} else {
    console.log(game + ' is not a masterpiece');
}
// superItalianBrosTwo is not a masterpiece
```

3. I consider a game to be a mediocre game if the score is anywhere between 30 and 80. *The Last Defender* was a mediocre game. But it was not a bad one. Hint: Writing out complex conditions in plain English helps.

```
var game = 'theLastDefender';
```

```
var score = donkeysGameScores[game];
if (score >= 80) {
    console.log(game + ' was a fun game');
} else if (score > 80 && score > 30) {
    console.log(game + ' was an ok game');
} else {
    console.log(game + ' was a bad game');
}
```

CODER'S CHECKLIST » Let's review the topics we covered

Pay special attention to equality operators, logical operators, and if . . . else if . . . else conditional statements. It will carry you through your entire programming experience. Here's what you learned in this chapter.

- Equality and comparison operators
- Logical operators
- Data validation using typeof and instanceof operators
- if . . . else if . . . else conditional statements

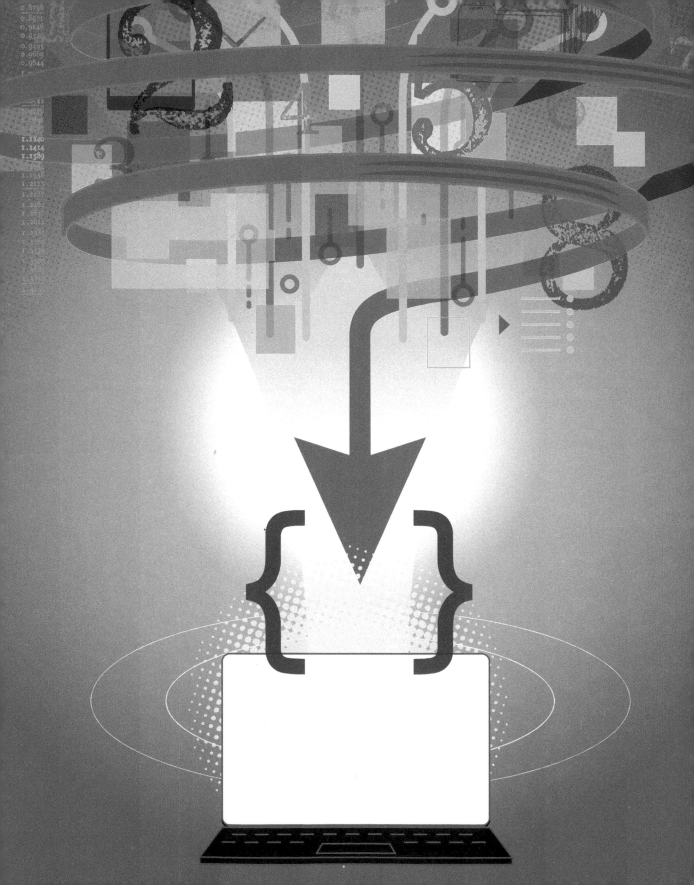

CHAPTER 5

Loops

Loops are one of the most powerful concepts in the programming world. Loops are how you tell a computer to repeat a set of operations as many times as needed.

Why Are Loops Used?

Loops are used when the number of times an operation should be performed is unknown, but you know when you should stop.

Humans think in loops as well—you just don't realize it! Stop to think for a minute about how you would count money. Imagine opening up your wallet or purse. Now, imagine there is physical money in there. How would you count the total dollar amount?

Working with computers is all about understanding the rules behind an operation. For convenience, let's write out the rules involved in counting money:

1. Collect your stack of bills.
2. Inspect each bill, one by one.
3. Mentally track the total as you continue to count. Add the value, bill by bill.
4. Stop counting after all bills have been inspected.

The last rule is the most important one to understand. Over the course of your life, how many bills have been in your wallet? Yesterday, you had five bills. So why isn't the rule "Stop after counting five bills"? Because the number of bills is not guaranteed to be any specific amount. So you can't use a specific number as a rule. In order to be flexible and have the rule accommodate for any number of bills, you can only say when you should stop counting.

Once you learn about **while** and **for** loops, you can write code using this style of logic that a computer can understand.

While Loops

A **while loop** is one type of loop that exists in JavaScript.

```
while (condition) {
}
```

A while loop will keep repeating until the condition evaluates to **false**.

STOPPING A LOOP

The condition in a loop is also referred to as the **terminating condition** of the loop. A loop is stopped by intentionally leading it to a **false** value. Once the value is **false**, the loop will end and the rest of the code beneath the loop will continue operating.

Loop Logic

The rules of counting money can help you with the logic. But now you need to figure out the operations that a computer can actually perform.

First, get a wallet full of bills. But the concept of a wallet does not exist in JavaScript. Instead, you would have an array of bills.

After checking your wallet, you see two $1 bills, one $5 bill, one $10 bill, and one $20 bill. So, your array of bills would look like this.

```
var bills = [1, 1, 5, 10, 20];
```

This is where it gets a little tricky. As programmers, we need to use a computer's rules. This requires a little creativity. This is how you can modify them:

1. Create an array of bills.
2. Access the value of each item in the array, by its index.
3. Create a variable that will accumulate its value from each item in the array.
4. Create a variable whose purpose is to get each item in the array by its index. Increment after each bill.
5. While the index variable is still within the bounds of the array, keep repeating.

Iteration

Before counting, write a loop that prints out each bill. Also validate the index.

Prep Work

Prepare the array of bills and declaration of the index, which starts at 0.

```
// array of bills
var bills = [1, 1, 5, 10, 20];
// index to access array values
var index = 0;
```

Terminating Condition: The Length Property

Remember the earlier discussion about the **length** property on arrays? It is the key to all the magic. The number output of **length** will change based on the size of the array. This will tell you how large the array is without you doing any extra work!

```
bills.length; // 5
```

As the loop operates, the index and length of the array is compared. While the index value is less than the length of the array, it is implied that the loop is still within the bounds of the array.

```
// our terminating condition
index < bills.length;
```

While **index < bills.length** continues to be **true**, the loop should continue.

```
// array of bills
var bills = [1, 1, 5, 10, 20];
// index to access array values
var index = 0;
// terminating condition
while (index < bills.length) {
    // increment index to eventually meet our terminating condition
    index++;
}
```

You now have a code loop that will terminate. But nothing interesting is happening inside. Before solving your original problem, confirm things are working with a **console.log** statement.

```
// array of bills
var bills = [1, 1, 5, 10, 20];
// index to access array values
var index = 0;
// terminating condition
while (index < bills.length) {
    var currentBill = bills[index];
    var indexPrint = 'I am on index' + index;
    console.log(indexPrint);

    var printedBill = 'I am currently on a $' + currentBill + 'bill!';
    console.log(printedBill);

    // increment index to eventually meet our terminating condition
    index++;
}
```

Place this code in a file and run it.

```
TERMINAL    PROBLEMS    OUTPUT    DEBUG CONSOLE                          1: bash           ∨

yueha@DESKTOP-MBVNIFF MINGW64 ~/repos/js-coding-for-teens/Chapters/5-Loops (master)
$ node codeSnippets.js
I am on index 0
I am currently on a $1 bill!
I am on index 1
I am currently on a $1 bill!
I am on index 2
I am currently on a $5 bill!
I am on index 3
I am currently on a $10 bill!
I am on index 4
I am currently on a $20 bill!
```

Excellent! The loop is working as expected.

UNDERSTANDING EACH ITERATION

A common way to refer to looping is the word **iterate**. One of the best ways to understand loops is to figure out what the values of the variables are upon each iteration. As your programming ability matures, it becomes easy to do the mental gymnastics in your head. But it's always nice to have a visual representation. If you ever find yourself unsure about what is happening in the loop, write a table to keep track of all of the values as your loop continues to run.

```
var bills = [1, 1, 5, 10, 20];
var index = 0;
while (index < bills.length) {
    console.log(bills[index]);
    index++;
}
```

ITERATION	INDEX	CONDITION	BILLS[INDEX]	BILLS
1	0	0 < 5	1	[1, 1, 5, 10, 20]
2	1	1 < 5	1	[1, 1, 5, 10, 20]
3	2	2 < 5	5	[1, 1, 5, 10, 20]
4	3	3 < 5	10	[1, 1, 5, 10, 20]
5	4	4 < 5	20	[1, 1, 5, 10, 20]

Before attempting iteration 6, the code checks 5 < 5, which is **false**. It stops and any code beneath the loop is finally run.

For Loops

A **while loop** is a great entry point into loops, but the **for loop** is more commonly used. It covers the most common situations with concise syntax.

STRUCTURE

The syntax is as follows. Note the semicolons.

```
for (initialization; condition; after) {
}
```

1. Initialization: The operation performed before any iteration. This is only performed once.
2. Condition: The terminating condition that is checked right before the next iteration.
3. After: The operation performed after an iteration. This is performed after event iteration.

WHILE LOOP VS. FOR LOOP SYNTAX

Let's revisit the strategy to iterate over an array in a while loop, in pseudo code.

```
initialize index
while (index is less than array.length) {
    increment index
}
```

1. Initialize variable to track index
2. Terminating condition
3. Increment index variable

A **for** loop takes these operations and squashes them onto a single line. Each operation is separated by a semicolon.

```
for (initialize index; index is less than array.length; increment index) {
}
```

The previous **while** loop example can be written as a **for** loop.

```
var bills = [1, 1, 5, 10, 20];
var index = 0;
while (index < bills.length) {
```

```
      console.log(bills[index]);
      index++;
}
```
It's all the same, just shorter.
```
var bills = [1, 1, 5, 10, 20];
for (var index = 0; index < bills.length; index++) {
      console.log(bills[index]);
}
```

Loop Modifying Keywords

There are algorithms where it makes sense to either skip subsequent operations in an iteration and move to the next iteration or outright leave the loop.

CONTINUE

Once a **continue** statement is found, the current iteration stops and progresses to the next. Let's change our prompt so we can use a **continue** in the solution.

Only print bills that are $5 or greater. How would that be expressed in code?
```
var bills = [1, 1, 5, 10, 20];
for (var index = 0; index < bills.length; index++) {
      if (bills[index] >= 5) {
            console.log(bills[index]);
      }
}
```
Simple stuff. But you can use a **continue** statement to solve the same challenge. This is what the pseudo code would look like.
```
for (loop over each bill) {
      if the bill is less than 5 dollars, skip everything beneath this statement
      print the bill
}
```
If the iteration stops when the bill is less than $5, it is implied that the bill won't be printed. In real code, it would look like this.
```
var bills = [1, 1, 5, 10, 20];
for (var index = 0; index < bills.length; index++) {
      // if the bill is less than 5 dollars
      if (bills[index] < 5) {
            // skip
            continue;
```

```
    }
    console.log(bills[index]);
  }
```

The output is as expected. The first two values in the array are ignored because they are less than 5. The loop never operates `console.log` because the `continue` statement inside the conditional prematurely stops the iteration.

```
TERMINAL   PROBLEMS   OUTPUT   DEBUG CONSOLE                              1: bash            ∨

yueha@DESKTOP-MBVNIFF MINGW64 ~/repos/js-coding-for-teens/Chapters/5-Loops (master)
$ node billPrint.js
5
10
20
```

BREAK

The keyword `continue` skips the subsequent operations inside a loop. But what if you want to cancel the loop completely? A **break** statement stops the current iteration in the same way `continue` does. But **break** goes even further and stops all subsequent iterations, too!

Now, change the prompt one more time. If you see a $5 bill, stop printing. This can be done without a **break** statement. But using one makes the algorithm easier to understand.

```
for (loop over each bill) {
    if the bill is equal to 5 dollars, exit loop
    print the bill
```

In real code, it would look like this.

```
var bills = [1, 1, 5, 10, 20];
for (var index = 0; index < bills.length; index++) {
    // if the bill is 5 dollars
    if (bills[index] === 5) {
        // exit loop completely
        break;
    }
    console.log(bills[index]);
}
```

```
TERMINAL   PROBLEMS   OUTPUT   DEBUG CONSOLE                              1: bash            ∨

yueha@DESKTOP-MBVNIFF MINGW64 ~/repos/js-coding-for-teens/Chapters/5-Loops (master)
$ node billPrint.js
1
1
```

Excellent! Just what you would expect. Once the code sees a 5, the loop stops.

Loops in Action

So far, you have spent the entire time making sure you understand how to cycle through all the bills in the array. It's time to solve the original prompt: Count the total amount in your wallet!

LOOP

Revisiting your previous code, no behavior inside. But the loop is prepared to iterate over the array of bills.

```
var bills = [1, 1, 5, 10, 20];
for (var i = 0; i < bills.length; i++) {
}
```

The variable **index** is shortened to **i**. This is the common variable name when tracking **index** in a loop.

In order to track the amount of money, a variable is needed. The value will start at **0**, because your loop has not counted any money yet.

```
var total = 0;
```

This type of variable is commonly referred to as an **accumulator**. It will progressively increase in value after every iteration of our loop. It "accumulates" value after each bill is visited.

Putting it all together, the value of each bill by index increases the value of **total**, the accumulator.

```
var bills = [1, 1, 5, 10, 20];
var total = 0;
for (var i = 0; i < bills.length; i++) {
    var currentValue = bills[i];
    total += currentValue;
```

```
}
console.log(total);
```
To make sure you have a full understanding of what is happening, let's create another table that represents each iteration.

ITERATION	I	CONDITION	CURRENTVALUE	TOTAL	BILLS
1	0	0 < 5	1	1	[1, 1, 5, 10, 20]
2	1	1 < 5	1	2	[1, 1, 5, 10, 20]
3	2	2 < 5	5	7	[1, 1, 5, 10, 20]
4	3	3 < 5	10	17	[1, 1, 5, 10, 20]
5	4	4 < 5	20	37	[1, 1, 5, 10, 20]

Crack the Code

Some very important concepts have been introduced in this chapter. Before moving on, make sure you have full confidence in your answers to the following questions. This is important, because moving forward, loops will be used extensively.

1. Why is a terminating condition important when working with loops?
2. When iterating over an array using a for loop, a variable, usually **i**, is initialized to the value **0**. What is the purpose of this variable when used as part of the loop terminating condition?
3. When iterating over an array using a **for** loop, a variable, usually **i**, is initialized to the value **0**. What is its purpose when used on the array inside the loop?
4. Write a table for the following loop.

```
var dogBreeds = ['pug', 'golden retriever', 'german shepherd'];
for (var i = 0; i < dogBreeds.length; i++) {
    var breed = dogBreeds[i];
    console.log(breed);
}
```

ITERATION	I	CONDITION	BREED

5. Write a table for the following loop.

```javascript
var gamers = ['super', 'smurf', 'sleepy', 'moth'];
for (var i = 0; i < gamers.length; i++) {
    var gamer = gamers[i];
    console.log(gamer);
}
```

ITERATION	I	CONDITION	GAMER

6. Write a table for the following loop. Note the nonstandard incrementor, `i += 2`.

```javascript
for (var i = 0; i < 7; i += 2) {
    console.log(i);
}
```

ITERATION	I	CONDITION

Debugging

Here's a quick reminder that it helps to run the code in the terminal. Seeing is believing.

1. The loop is not printing the cat breeds.

```javascript
var catBreeds = [
    'Maine Coon',
    'ragdoll'
];
for (var i = 0; i < catBreeds; i++) {
    console.log(catBreeds[i]);
}
```

2. The loop is not printing the bills.

```
var bills = [1, 5, 10, 20, 50];
for (var i = 0; i > bills.length; i++) {
    console.log(bills[i]);
}
```

3. The loop is iterating one too many times. The last value printed is **undefined**.
```
var hangmanLetters = ['d', 'a', 'r', 'k', 's', 'o', 'u', 'l', 's'];
for (var i = 0; i <= hangmanLetters.length; i++) {
    console.log(hangmanLetters[i]);
}
```

4. The loop is not printing the cat names.
```
var catNames = ['Pegasus', 'Maximillion', 'Joey'];
for (var i; i < catNames.length; i++) {
    console.log(catNames[i]);
}
```

5. The loop should be skipping data if the entry in the array is a string. I am trying to use **continue** to skip the loop's operations prematurely. But my loop is still printing out all of the data.
```
var mixedDataTypes = ['a', 30, 'b', 'd', 'd', 1, 3];
for (var i = 0; i < mixedDataTypes.length; i++) {
    var currData = mixedDataTypes[i];
    console.log(currData);
    if (typeof currData === 'string') {
        continue;
    }
}
```

CODER'S CHECKLIST » Let's review the topics we covered

To be successful in JavaScript, it is incredibly important to understand loops. Programs of all sizes extensively use them to solve challenging problems. Here's what you learned in this chapter:

- Terminating conditions
- While loops
- For loops
- Premature skipping of an interaction: continue
- Complete exit of the entire loop: break

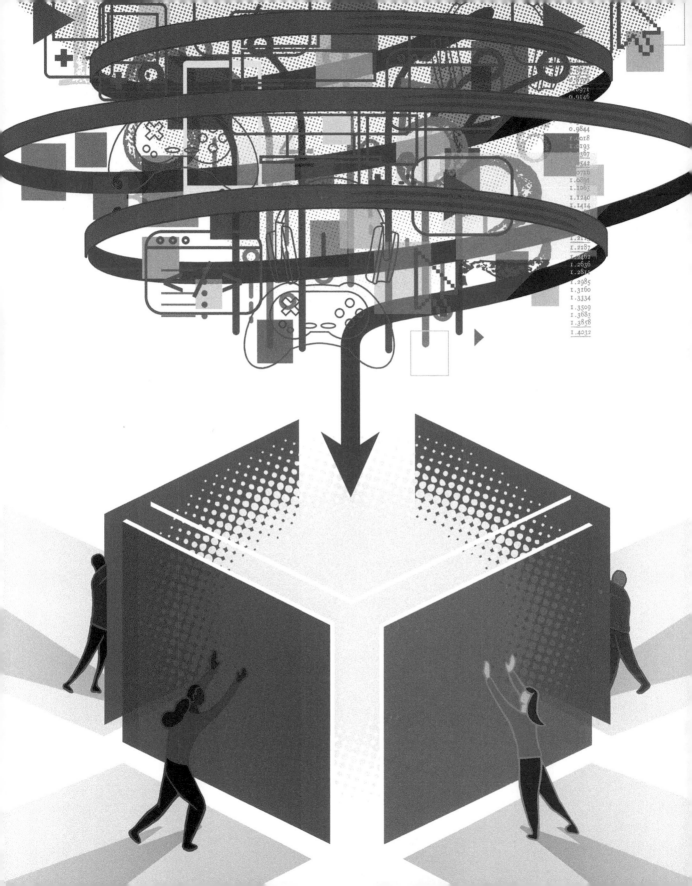

CHAPTER 6

Functions

By this point you have been introduced to `console.log` and `prompt.question`. These are **functions**, and now you are finally equipped to learn more about them! Functions are a way of grouping a collection of statements together to perform a task. They are for data manipulation, exhibiting behavior, calculations—anything you can imagine. For the purposes of this book, functions have names and are run with parentheses to initiate their designed behavior. `console.log` is a function that has already been made for you. But now you are ready to write your own.

Why Are Functions Used?

Functions have multiple aspects that make them useful to programmers. They are a core part of programming. They'll be some of the first tools you'll reach for when solving problems. Programming challenges that are hard become manageable. Challenges that are near impossible can become a reality.

REUSE CODE

Does `console.log` get destroyed after it is used? Absolutely not! Functions can be used as many or as few times as you want. Often, when a programmer sees two of the same kinds of operations, they figure out strategies to reduce the amount of code that would need to be repeatedly rewritten. Functions are the go-to strategy for this.

ABSTRACTION

If the skin of `console.log` were peeled back and you were able to look at how it's implemented, you would see something incredibly complex. `console.log` is a fantastic

abstraction. It performs a complex operation using a simple command. Some programmers worked very hard to make `console.log` and let the world use it in an easy way.

SOLVE LARGE CHALLENGES

Mainstream programs are dauntingly complex. Humans do not have the mental capacity to figure out the entire solution to complex problems in their heads. Instead, your brain breaks down large challenges into many smaller challenges. You solve each small challenge one by one and package it up. You then combine all of these small solutions to solve the problem at hand. Functions are perfect for this.

Function Creation

There are two ways to declare a function. The two are similar and you don't have to worry too much about the nuances between them. But as a JavaScript programmer, you will be using both, depending on the situation.

FUNCTION DECLARATION

The first syntax is to have the keyword **function** and the name after it. A semicolon is optional. This declaration style will be used almost exclusively.

```
function functionNameOfYourChoosing() {
    // code here
}
```

FUNCTION EXPRESSION

The second syntax has the keyword **function** assigned to a variable, using the declaration **var**. A semicolon is recommended. This declaration style will be used only when working with **object-oriented programming**.

```
var functionNameOfYourChoosing = function () {
    // code here
};
```

Function Invocation

Parentheses on the end of the function name run the operations inside it. The formal term is **invoke**. This syntax is identical for both types of function declarations.

```
functionNameOfYourChoosing();
```

Return Statement

Natively, a function does not expose data that it has computed to the outside world.

```
function add() {
    var computed = 5 + 5;
}
add(); // undefined
```

That's because you have not told JavaScript that you want it! Using the keyword **return**, a function can expose a piece of data.

```
function add() {
    var computed = 5 + 5
    return computed
}
add(); // 10
```

Function Parameters

In the previous example, the **add** function can only add 5 and 5 together. Wouldn't it be nicer if you could take any two numbers and add them together? This is where **parameters** come into play.

Parameters are pre-prepared variables. This allows functions to fit many situations.

```
function add(num1, num2) {
    return num1 + num2;
}
```

You have told JavaScript that two variables, **num1** and **num2**, can be passed in during invocation. With parameters, this **add** function handles any numbers.

```
add(10, 5); // 15
add(20, 30); // 50
```

Early Termination with Return

The keyword **return** actually serves two purposes at once.
1. It outputs a value from a function.
2. It stops the function execution.

You may find yourself not wanting to execute code after a certain point or to make a decision and cease all subsequent operations.

PROTECT ADD FROM TYPE COERCION

Let's spruce up your **add** function and protect it from bad inputs. Remember type coercion and the plus operator?

```
function add(num1, num2) {
    return num1 + num2;
}
add('10', '5'); // '105'
add(20, '30'); // '2030'
```

Your addition function can **string concatenate**. But you always want to add, or at least attempt to. Let's protect it with an early **return**. If data are used that are not numbers, the function should **return NaN**.

```
function add(num1, num2) {
    // if num1 is not a number OR num2 is not a number
    if (typeof num1 !== 'number' || typeof num2 !== 'number') {
        return NaN;
    }
    return num1 + num2;
}
add('10', 5); // 'NaN'
add(20, '30'); // 'NaN'
```

Using an early **return**, you have protected the function from type coercion or any other bad inputs.

Scope

Now would be a good time to talk about how variable availability works when using functions. In coding terms, variable availability is referred to as **scope**. Moving forward, functions will be written extensively. It is important to understand if a particular piece of data you need is available in a particular section of your code.

VAR: FUNCTION SCOPED

The location of declaration now matters. A declared variable inside a function is available exclusively within the function itself.

This code will give unexpected behavior.

```
function sampleFunc() {
    var innerVariable = 'I am only available inside this function';
    console.log(innerVariable);
}
function otherSampleFunc() {
    console.log(innerVariable);
}
sampleFunc();
otherSampleFunc();
```

```
TERMINAL    PROBLEMS    OUTPUT    DEBUG CONSOLE                                    1: bash           ∨

yueha@DESKTOP-MBVNIFF MINGW64 ~/repos/js-coding-for-teens/Chapters/5-Loops (master)
$ node codeSnippets.js
I am only available inside this function
C:\Users\yueha\repos\js-coding-for-teens\Chapters\5-Loops\codeSnippets.js:7
    console.log(innerVariable);
                ^

ReferenceError: innerVariable is not defined
    at otherSampleFunc (C:\Users\yueha\repos\js-coding-for-teens\Chapters\5-Loops\codeSnippets.js:7:17)
    at Object.<anonymous> (C:\Users\yueha\repos\js-coding-for-teens\Chapters\5-Loops\codeSnippets.js:11:1)
    at Module._compile (internal/modules/cjs/loader.js:959:30)
    at Object.Module._extensions..js (internal/modules/cjs/loader.js:995:10)
    at Module.load (internal/modules/cjs/loader.js:815:32)
    at Function.Module._load (internal/modules/cjs/loader.js:727:14)
    at Function.Module.runMain (internal/modules/cjs/loader.js:1047:10)
    at internal/main/run_main_module.js:17:11
```

An error occurs when running `otherSampleFunc()`. This is a consequence of how JavaScript implements scope.

LEXICAL SCOPE

Different programming languages have their own rules when it comes to scope. JavaScript uses **lexical scope**. Lexical scope is when variables are available within itself and its inner scopes, but not in outer scopes. Let's look at some examples.

Functions Inside Functions

Functions can be written inside other functions! This creates two tiers of scope. One is an **inner scope** and the other is an **outer scope**.

Variables declared in the outer scope are available in any inner scopes.

```javascript
function outerScopeFunc() {
    var outerVar = 'I am outer scoped! I exist in both scopes';
    function innerScopeFunc() {
        console.log(outerVar);
    }
    innerScopeFunc();
}
outerScopeFunc();
```

```
TERMINAL    PROBLEMS    OUTPUT    DEBUG CONSOLE                         1: bash          ∨

yueha@DESKTOP-MBVNIFF MINGW64 ~/repos/js-coding-for-teens/Chapters/5-Loops (master)
$ node codeSnippets.js
I am outer scoped! I exist in both scopes
```

But inner scopes are not available in scopes above themselves.

```javascript
function outerScopeFunc() {
    function innerScopeFunc() {
        var innerVar = 'I am inner scoped! I only exist inside here';
    }
    console.log(innerVar);
    innerScopeFunc();
}
outerScopeFunc();
```

```
TERMINAL    PROBLEMS    OUTPUT    DEBUG CONSOLE                         1: bash          ∨

yueha@DESKTOP-MBVNIFF MINGW64 ~/repos/js-coding-for-teens/Chapters/5-Loops (master)
$ node codeSnippets.js
C:\Users\yueha\repos\js-coding-for-teens\Chapters\5-Loops\codeSnippets.js:5
    console.log(innerVar);
                ^

ReferenceError: innerVar is not defined
```

Understanding scope is key to writing functions. Sometimes the variable won't be available where it is needed and vice versa. Always be mindful of scope.

Esports Player Performance

Working with functions empowers you to solve hard challenges in elegant ways. Let's take a big leap forward in your problem-solving abilities! Electro is a world-class Esports team for *Undersea*, a popular computer game. They have an excellent record on the global stage. With a rich roster of talented players, they rotate who plays and who sits on the sidelines. Players who do not participate in a match are referred to as "benched" players.

DID A PLAYER PARTICIPATE?

Your first challenge will be checking player participation in a tournament. This function should be able to handle any possible player and for any tournament results. They have to be **parameters**. Let's call the function **playedInTournament** and the two parameters **tournament** and **player**.

```
function playedInTournament(tournament, player) {
}
```

For this exercise, the **tournament** parameter will have the following structure. It is an object data structure with one key: **players**. The value associated with the key is an array of player names.

```
{
    players: ['smirk', 'knight', 'fly']
};
```

Now you need to find if a player has played in a tournament. There is a **players** key in the object. The goal is to check if that player exists in the array. Immediately, you know a **for** loop is needed. The array is nested in the object, so it must be accessed by its key name, **players**. There also needs to be a check if the player has played in the game. Thinking in programming terms, this needs an **if** condition.

```
function playedInTournament(tournament, player) {
    var players = tournament.players;
    for (var i = 0; i < players.length; i++) {
        var currentPlayer = players[i];
        if (currentPlayer === player) {
        }
    }
}
```

If the **currentPlayer** is the player to check, **return true**. But when should **false** be returned? If the check has exhausted all players in the array, that implies the player has not been found at all. At the very end of the function, **return false**.

```
// tournament.js
function playedInTournament(tournament, player) {
    var players = tournament.players;
    for (var i = 0; i < players.length; i++) {
        var currentPlayer = players[i];
        if (currentPlayer === player) {
            return true;
        }
    }
    return false;
}
```

It's time to validate the code. To do so, you will need a **console.log** in order to have the data from the function appear in the terminal. I named the file **tournament.js**.

```
var sampleTournament = {
    win: true,
    players: ['smirk', 'knight', 'fly']
};
console.log(playedInTournament(sampleTournament, 'smirk'));
console.log(playedInTournament(sampleTournament, 'superb'));
```

TERMINAL   PROBLEMS   OUTPUT   DEBUG CONSOLE   1: bash   ⌄

```
yueha@DESKTOP-MBVNIFF MINGW64 ~/repos/js-coding-for-teens/exercises/ch6 (master)
$ node tournament.js
true
false
```

Looks good! In the `sampleTournament` object, smirk played but superb did not. Remove the two `console.log` statements and the data structure `sampleTournament` from the file. Moving forward, they will not be necessary.

DATA STRUCTURES INSIDE DATA STRUCTURES

For subsequent exercises, a list of tournament results is required. Inside each tournament result, we also need a list of players who participated in the tournament. Add this data structure to the file.

```
var tournaments = [
    { win: true, players: ['smirk', 'knight', 'fly'] },
    { win: true, players: ['superb', 'san', 'tired'] },
    { win: true, players: ['smirk', 'knight', 'tired'] },
    { win: false, players: ['san', 'superb', 'fly'] },
    { win: true, players: ['smirk', 'san', 'fly'] },
    { win: false, players: ['superb', 'knight', 'tired'] },
];
```

NUMBER OF TOURNAMENTS PLAYED

The data about player participation is inside the array of tournaments. With an array of data, there is a clear need for a loop.

```
function tournamentsPlayed(tournaments, player) {
    var playCount = 0;
    for (var i = 0; i < tournaments.length; i++) {
        var currentTournament = tournaments[i];
    }
    return playCount;
}
```

This time, you need to check to see if the player participated in the tournament. Not only that, but you have to keep track of the number of times this has occurred. Figuring out if a player played in a particular tournament is a lot of work. Each tournament entry needs to have the inner array searched. But this has already been solved in `playedInTournament`. The function can be reused instead.

```
        var currentTournament = tournaments[i];
        var playerDidPlay = playedInTournament(currentTournament, player);
        if (playerDidPlay) {
            playCount += 1;
        }
    }
```

Validate the code by running it with `console.log`.

```
console.log(tournamentsPlayed(tournaments, 'smirk'));
console.log(tournamentsPlayed(tournaments, 'superb'));
```

```
TERMINAL    PROBLEMS    OUTPUT    DEBUG CONSOLE                                      1: bash                  ˅

yueha@DESKTOP-MBVNIFF MINGW64 ~/repos/js-coding-for-teens/exercises/ch6 (master)
$ node tournament.js
3
3
```

Looks good. Both smirk and superb played in three tournaments. These console.log statements can be removed now.

NUMBER OF TOURNAMENTS WON

Now, take it one step further. Check and see the number of times a particular player has participated in a tournament where the team won. To do so clearly, you will need:

1. A loop
2. An accumulator variable to track the number of tournaments won

```
function tournamentsWon(tournaments, player) {
    var winCount = 0;
    for (var i = 0; i < tournaments.length; i++) {
        var currentTournament = tournaments[i];
    }
    return winCount;
}
```

Things are a little different compared to **gamesPlayed**. Two conditions are necessary:

1. The player participated in the tournament
2. The team won

Luckily, **playedInTournament** can be used for the first condition. For the second, each entry has the tournament result, in the key **win**. You need both to be **true** in order to count the game as a tournament win when that particular player participated. In this case, the AND operator, **&&**, is used to assert both at once.

```
function tournamentsWon(tournaments, player) {
    var winCount = 0;
    for (var i = 0; i < tournaments.length; i++) {
        var currentTournament = tournaments[i];
        var playerDidPlay = playedInTournament(currentTournament, player);
        var tournamentWon = currentTournament.win;
```

```
        if (playerDidPlay && tournamentWon) {
            winCount += 1;
        }
    }
    return winCount;
}
```

Validate the code with a **console.log**.

```
console.log(tournamentsWon(tournaments, 'smirk'));
console.log(tournamentsWon(tournaments, 'superb'));
```

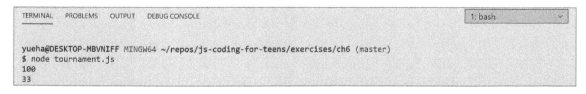

Looks good! It looks like smirk has won three tournaments and superb has won one.

PLAYER WIN RATE

Now you are interested in determining the win rates. To solve this, divide the number of wins by the number of tournaments played.

$$\frac{(\text{tournaments won})}{(\text{total tournaments participated})} \times 100$$

The algorithm that needs to be written is easy, because both have already been solved! For a cleaner output, **parseInt** will be used. It turns a decimal number into a whole number.

```
function playerWinRate(tournaments, player) {
    var total = tournamentsPlayed(tournaments, player);
    var won = tournamentsWon(tournaments, player);
    var percentage = (won / total) * 100;
    return parseInt(percentage);
}
```

Let's validate.

```
console.log(playerWinRate(tournaments, 'smirk'));
console.log(playerWinRate(tournaments, 'superb'));
```

```
TERMINAL    PROBLEMS    OUTPUT    DEBUG CONSOLE                                          1: bash              ˅

yueha@DESKTOP-MBVNIFF MINGW64 ~/repos/js-coding-for-teens/exercises/ch6 (master)
$ node tournament.js
100
33
```

It appears smirk has a perfect win rate, while superb is at 33 percent.

WHO SHOULD PLAY?

Oh no! It looks like there is a dispute between two players. It appears smirk and superb both want to play in the next tournament, but there is room for only one more player. To resolve this, management has decided to check the performance of the team when each respective player was participating. Management are not programmers and they don't want to see two numbers. They want to see a well-structured message on who should play and who should be benched.

So far, you've solved a multitude of challenges. Many simple functions have been written and composed together to solve tough challenges. Last one to go!

There is already a function to calculate the win rate of each player. Just compare win rates to discover who should be in the next tournament. This time around, three parameters are required:

1. The team's tournament performances and its active players in each tournament
2. A player
3. Another player to compare

Immediately, you know you need each player's win rates.

```
function whoShouldPlay(tournaments, player1, player2) {
    var player1WinRate = playerWinRate(tournaments, player1);
    var player2WinRate = playerWinRate(tournaments, player2);
}
```

This time, you will want to print out two nice messages. Keep track of who will be the **benchedPlayer** and who will be the **activePlayer**. If **player1** has a better win rate, they should be the **activePlayer** and **player2** should be the **benchedPlayer**.

```
function whoShouldPlay(tournaments, player1, player2) {
    var player1WinRate = playerWinRate(tournaments, player1);
    var player2WinRate = playerWinRate(tournaments, player2);
    var benchedPlayer;
    var activePlayer;
    if (player1WinRate > player2WinRate) {
        activePlayer = player1;
        benchedPlayer = player2;
    }
}
```

But that's not enough, because the opposite situation needs to be handled. In this situation, you don't need an **else if**. There are only two options. An **else** statement will work perfectly fine.

For the sake of management's requirements, add a **console.log** for each player's status with a good message.

```javascript
function whoShouldPlay(tournaments, player1, player2) {
    var player1WinRate = playerWinRate(tournaments, player1);
    var player2WinRate = playerWinRate(tournaments, player2);
    var benchedPlayer;
    var activePlayer;
    if (player1WinRate > player2WinRate) {
        activePlayer = player1;
        benchedPlayer = player2;
    } else {
        activePlayer = player2;
        benchedPlayer = player1;
    }
    console.log(activePlayer + ' should play in the next tournament');
    console.log(benchedPlayer + ' should be benched');
}
whoShouldPlay(tournaments, 'smirk', 'superb');
```

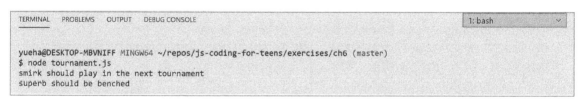

```
TERMINAL    PROBLEMS    OUTPUT    DEBUG CONSOLE                                    1: bash            ∨

yueha@DESKTOP-MBVNIFF MINGW64 ~/repos/js-coding-for-teens/exercises/ch6 (master)
$ node tournament.js
smirk should play in the next tournament
superb should be benched
```

The results are in and the difference is clear. Looks like smirk is the better player and superb will be benched.

RECAP

This exercise was an integration of every technical aspect of JavaScript that you have learned so far. But you may have noticed that your approach to solving the problem is just as important. You took one large challenge and deconstructed it into five easier challenges:
1. Compare win rates between two players.
2. Calculate win rate of a player.
3. Calculate total games played by a player.
4. Calculate games won by a player.
5. Inspect whether a player was in a tournament.

The sum of all these parts created a simple solution to a complex problem.

Crack the Code

This chapter is a two-for-one deal. Not only did you learn about functions, you also got a small taste of the types of strategies that programmers use to solve challenging problems in a simple way.

1. What qualities make functions desirable to use when programming?
2. What keyword does a function need to have in order to output a value that is exposed outside of the function?
3. What does a function output if there is no explicit return?
4. What is scope?
5. What type of scope does JavaScript use? Explain in your own words.

Debugging

Programmers have a secret weapon called **unit testing**. Breaking down problems allows you to check the correctness of code in small increments. Each function is small, so it is easy to test. If every small function works, the challenge as a whole should work with no problem!

```
// important! this function will not work for data structures
// and objects. Only strings, numbers, null, booleans, and undefined
function test(description, actual, expected) {
    console.log(description);
    if (actual === expected) {
        console.log('  pass!');
    } else {
        console.log('  fail!');
        console.log('    received: ', actual);
        console.log('    expected: ', expected);
    }
}
```

Here is a very basic function that lets you:

1. Write a quick message to yourself about what will be tested.
2. Compare two values.
3. Know if you get what you expect. If not, you print what you computed versus what you were expecting.

Before you do your real debugging problem, it's time for you to put this test function into action. To do so, you'll create an intentionally incorrect **add** function and see what your test function gives you as output.

```
function add(num1, num2) {
    return num1 - num2;
}
test('add test #1', add(10, 20), 30);
test('add test #2', add(10, 15), 25);
```

Great! Not only did you let JavaScript check if your code is correct, but you also let it show you what you computed, if your function is wrong.

GUESS MY CAT'S NAME

Let's make a quick little game in your terminal using functions. This isn't easy! You will need to break down the problem into many sub-problems and encapsulate the algorithm in a function.

You will type in a character and then you will receive feedback on the progress of your guess. Once you have correctly guessed all of the characters, the full name will be printed and the program will exit.

Right now, your program isn't working very well. In fact, it's not working at all. Here is your broken code:

```javascript
var prompt = require("readline-sync");
// important! this function will not work for data structures
// and objects. Only strings, numbers, null, booleans, and undefined
function test(description, actual, expected) {
    console.log(description);
    if (actual === expected) {
        console.log('  pass!');
    } else {
        console.log('  fail!');
        console.log('    received: ', actual);
        console.log('    expected: ', expected);
    }
}
function includes(arrOrStr, item) {
    for (var i = 0; i < arrOrStr.length; i++) {
        var currItem = arrOrStr[i];
        if (currItem !== item) {
            return true;
        }
    }
    return false;
}
test('includes #1', includes('cat', 'a'), true);
test('includes #2', includes('cat', 't'), true);
test('includes #3', includes('cat', 'f'), false);
function createHint(actualName, allUserGuesses) {
    var output = '';
    for (var i = 0; i < actualName.length; i++) {
        var currChar = actualName[i];
        if (includes(allUserGuesses, currChar)) {
            output += currChar + ' ';
        } else {
            output = '_ ';
        }
    }
    return output;
}
// note the space at the end of the expected values!
```

```
test('createHint #1', createHint('charlie', 'chle'), 'c h _ _ l _ e ');
test('createHint #2', createHint('cat', 'u'), '_ _ _ ');
test('createHint #3', createHint('cat', 'a'), '_ a _ ');
function correctlyGuessed(actualName, allUserGuesses) {
    for (var i = 0; i < actualName.length; i++) {
        var currChar = actualName[i];
        if (includes(allUserGuesses, currChar)) {
            return false;
        }
    }
    return true;
}
test('correctlyGuessed #1', correctlyGuessed('charlie', 'chle'), false);
test('correctlyGuessed #2', correctlyGuessed('cat', 'tac'), true);
test('correctlyGuessed #3', correctlyGuessed('cat', 'cat'), true);
function isMultiCharGuess(guess) {
    return guess.length === 1;
}
test('isMultiCharGuess #1', isMultiCharGuess('a'), false);
test('isMultiCharGuess #2', isMultiCharGuess('av'), true);
test('isMultiCharGuess #3', isMultiCharGuess('c'), false);
function hangCat(catName) {
    var userGuesses = '';
    // infinite loop until we break out, after figuring out our cat name
    while (true) {
        var guess = prompt.question('What\'s my cat\'s name?\n');
        // prevent user from submitting multiple characters
        if (isMultiCharGuess(guess)) {
            console.log('only guess one character at a time!');
            continue;
        }
        // add to string of guessed characters
        userGuesses += guess;
        var isCorrect = correctlyGuessed(catName, userGuesses);
        if (isCorrect) {
            console.log('That is right! My cat is named ' + catName);
            // once name is found, exit loop
            break;
```

```
        } else {
              console.log('Nope! That is not my cat\'s name');
              console.log('The characters you have guessed are: '
+ userGuesses);
              console.log('Currently you have correctly guessed: ',
createHint(catName, userGuesses));
        }
    }
}
```
// uncomment after all of your tests pass
// hangCat('chappy');

Notice all of the test cases in this file? They're failing! Once you get them to pass, you can comment out all of your tests and uncomment the very last line of the file, and properly play your game. Good luck!

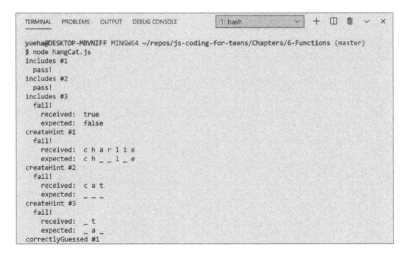

CODER'S CHECKLIST » Let's review the topics we covered

☐ Function syntax   ☐ Scope   ☐ Problem solving   ☐ Program testing

CHAPTER 7

Data Manipulation

So far, most of our time has been spent learning about various ways of working with data. But what is just as important is the ability to change data in order to solve interesting challenges. Sometimes information is in an object and you need to extract information from it and put it in an array.

Numbers, strings, arrays, and objects can all be modified in ways that help you solve challenges. Let's get started!

Numbers

Numbers are a very straightforward concept, so they don't have too much to them. They can be either slightly modified or converted to a string.

PARSEINT

The function **parseInt** takes a number and turns it into a whole number. It does not round up or down, technically. It removes the decimal places from the number. More importantly, however, it is a way of taking a stringified version of a number and converting the actual data type to a number.

```
parseInt(1322.23423); // 1322
parseInt('1322.23423'); // 1322
```

PARSEFLOAT

In the same way **parseInt** parses a number and a string version of a number, **parseFloat** does, too, except it keeps all decimal values from the original number.

```
parseFloat(1322.23423); // 1322.23423
parseFloat('1322.23423'); // 1322.23423
```

Strings

Within the scope of this book, most string operations will be omitted. But there are still two important manipulations to be mindful of.

ACCESSING BY INDEX

For some algorithms, it is important to inspect a string, element by element. This can be accomplished by accessing each character by index. The way strings and arrays access elements, by index, is identical.

```
var dog = 'Misu';
dog[0]; // 'M'
dog[2]; // 's'
```

TOLOWERCASE AND TOUPPERCASE

To change the characters to all lower or all upper cases can be done using **toLowerCase** and **toUpperCase**, respectively.

```
var dog = 'Misu';
dog.toLowerCase(); // 'misu'
dog.toUpperCase(); // 'MISU'
```

Wait! Why is this function being used behind the variable name? Well, the function is technically a **method**. There will be a deep dive into the purpose and reason of this difference. For the time being, just know that methods are invoked with this syntax.

Arrays

Modifying **arrays** is so common that JavaScript includes many built-in operations to modify them in the ways we need.

INSERTION

Entries in an array are accessed by index.

```
var animals = ['dog', 'cat', 'horse', 'bird'];
animals[0]; // 'dog'
```

The same syntax to access an entry in an array can also be used to **reassign** a new value into an index.

```
var animals = ['dog', 'cat', 'horse', 'bird'];
animals[0] = 'pig';
animals[0]; // 'pig'
```

PUSH

A common operation is inserting at the end of an array. The array method name is **push**.

```
var sampleArray = [];
sampleArray.push(10);
sampleArray; // [10]
```

POP

Another common operation is the removal of the last entry in the array, using the method **pop**.

```
var sampleArray = [2, 10];
sampleArray.pop();
sampleArray; // [2]
```

SHIFT

The first element of an array can removed using the method **shift**.

```
var sampleArray = [2, 10];
sampleArray.shift();
sampleArray; // [10]
```

UNSHIFT

The last array operation is **unshift**, which inserts an element to the front of the array.

```
var sampleArray = [2, 10];
sampleArray.unshift(5);
sampleArray; // [5, 2, 10]
```

Objects

Compared to arrays, **objects** are not modified to the same extent. This is for more advanced, technical reasons. But objects still support insertion, replacement, and deletion.

INSERTION AND REPLACEMENT

Object value insertion is performed with the equal sign.

```
var animals = {};
animals.dog = 'sparky';
animals; // { dog: 'sparky' }
```

The syntax for insertion is the same as replace. If the key already exists, it will replace the value.

```
var animals = {
    dog: 'sparky'
};
animals.dog = 'not sparky';
animals; // { dog: 'not sparky' }
```

DELETION

Removing an element from an object is an uncommon operation. The **delete** operator removes a key-value pair in an object.

```
var animals = {
    dog: 'sparky'
};
delete animals.dog;
animals; // { }
```

Mutation

The idea of modifying a data type, as opposed to always making a new version, is referred to as **mutability**. An operation can be **mutative**, which means it modifies the existing data. A piece of data can also be referred to as **immutable**, which means it fundamentally cannot be modified.

In the below example, we did not assign or reassign to a new variable when using the array and object operations. That is because **push**, **pop**, **shift**, and **unshift** are operations that **mutate** the existing array. The operations that were shown are ones that change the existing data structure.

```
var animals = ['dog', 'cat', 'horse', 'bird'];
animals.push('lizard');
animals; // ['dog', 'cat', 'horse', 'bird', 'lizard'];
```

In fact, reassigning is a very bad thing. It can create very unintuitive code.

```
var animals = ['dog', 'cat', 'horse', 'bird'];
animals = animals.push('lizard');
animals; // 5
```

The **return** value is 5 because that is the length of the new array, after pushing **lizard** into it. But that probably is not the desired output. More likely than not, the desired output is the array itself.

STRINGS ARE IMMUTABLE

```
var animal = 'd';
animal += 'og';
animal; // 'dog
```

Have you noticed how you have been using the **reassign operator**? That's because strings are **immutable**. An existing string cannot be updated. It must be reassigned to create an entirely new string.

```
var animal = 'd';
animal + 'dog';
animal; // 'd'
```

Because of the fact that JavaScript's strings are immutable, string concatenation does not modify `animal`.

Data Manipulation in Action

It is much easier to understand data manipulation when you see it in action. We'll also go over the most common data manipulation strategies you will encounter. Let's get started!

BUILDING A NEW ARRAY

Taking an array and modifying it, in one form or another, is one of the most common operations in all programs. In many situations, it is more advantageous to build an entirely new array than to modify the existing one.

Given the following array, create an array of the names of players with a skill level that is higher than 5.

```
var players = [
    { name: 'superb', skill: 3 },
    { name: 'smirk', skill: 7 },
    { name: 'tired', skill: 6 },
    { name: 'ANS', skill: 9 }
];
```

This is the expected output.

```
['smirk', 'tired', 'ANS'];
```

To make the code more manageable, you will place the algorithm in a function. If there is an array of elements to inspect, a **for** loop should be your first thought.

```
function getSkilledPlayers(allPlayers) {
    for (var i = 0; i < allPlayers.length; i++) {
    }
}
```

Start with an empty array and continually **push** in players (if they are skilled) into it. The pseudo code would look something like this.

```
function getSkilledPlayers(allPlayers) {
    start with an empty array
    inspect each element, one by one
    if the player is skilled, add the player's name to the empty array
    return the new array
}
```

First, prep the loop, our empty array, and **return** value.

```
function getSkilledPlayers(allPlayers) {
    var skilledPlayers = [];
    for (var i = 0; i < allPlayers.length; i++) {
        var player = allPlayers[i]
    }
    return skilledPlayers;
}
```

You are interested in whether the player is of a certain caliber of skill. Clearly, a conditional is needed.

```
function getSkilledPlayers(allPlayers) {
    var skilledPlayers = [];
    for (var i = 0; i < allPlayers.length; i++) {
        var player = allPlayers[i]
        if (player.skill > 5) {
        }
    }
    return skilledPlayers;
}
```

HACKER HINT

If you find yourself needing to use the `delete` operator, it is more likely that your algorithm should be solved with an array instead.

So far, nothing is new. You have seen all of this logic before. But this time around, the array needs to be built up, one by one. If a particular player meets the criteria, **push** in their **name**.

```
function getSkilledPlayers(allPlayers) {
    var skilledPlayers = [];
    for (var i = 0; i < allPlayers.length; i++) {
        var player = allPlayers[i];
        if (player.skill > 5) {
            skilledPlayers.push(player.name);
        }
    }
    return skilledPlayers;
}
```
Putting it all together, this is your code and your expected output.
```
var players = [
    { name: 'superb', skill: 3 },
    { name: 'smirk', skill: 7 },
    { name: 'tired', skill: 6 },
    { name: 'ANS', skill: 9 }
];
function getSkilledPlayers(allPlayers) {
    var skilledPlayers = [];
    for (var i = 0; i < allPlayers.length; i++) {
        var player = allPlayers[i];
        if (player.skill > 5) {
            skilledPlayers.push(player.name);
        }
    }
    return skilledPlayers;
}
console.log(getSkilledPlayers(players));
```

TERMINAL   PROBLEMS   OUTPUT   DEBUG CONSOLE   1: bash   ∨

```
yueha@DESKTOP-MBVNIFF MINGW64 ~/repos/js-coding-for-teens/exercises/ch7 (master)
$ node skilledPlayers.js
[ 'smirk', 'tired', 'ANS' ]
```

For good measure, a table can be written to see how values are changing after each iteration.

ITERATION	PLAYER.NAME	PLAYER.SKILL	PLAYER.SKILL > 5	SKILLEDPLAYERS
				[]
1	superb	3	false	[]
2	smirk	7	true	['smirk']
3	tired	6	true	['smirk', 'tired']
4	ANS	9	true	['smirk', 'tired', 'ANS']

Updating Objects in an Array

Let's say you have an object where the keys are player names and their ages. It would make sense to merge the data into a single data structure. You can accomplish this using the strategies that you've learned.

```
var players = [
    { name: 'superb', skill: 3 },
    { name: 'smirk', skill: 7 },
    { name: 'tired', skill: 6 },
    { name: 'ANS', skill: 9 }
];
var playerAges = {
    superb: 21,
    smirk: 21,
    tired: 22,
    ANS: 21
};
```

This is the expected output.

```
[
    { name: 'superb', skill: 3, age: 21 },
    { name: 'smirk', skill: 7, age: 21 },
    { name: 'tired', skill: 6, age: 22 },
    { name: 'ANS', skill: 9, age: 21 }
];
```

Like the previous question, iteration is clearly needed.

```
function playerWithAges(players, ages) {
    var playerData = [];
    for (var i = 0; i < players.length; i++) {
```

```
        var player = players[i];
    }
    return playerData;
}
```

But this time, the **return** value is not an array of strings. It is an array of objects. Inside each iteration, create a new object with the data and **push** it into the array.

Putting it all together, the file and output should look like this.

```
var players = [
    { name: 'superb', skill: 3 },
    { name: 'smirk', skill: 7 },
    { name: 'tired', skill: 6 },
    { name: 'ANS', skill: 9 }
];
var playerAges = {
    superb: 21,
    smirk: 21,
    tired: 22,
    ANS: 21
};
function playerWithAges(players, ages) {
    var playerData = [];
    for (var i = 0; i < players.length; i++) {
        var player = players[i];
        var playerEntry = {
            name: player.name,
            skill: player.skill,
            age: ages[player.name]
        };
        playerData.push(playerEntry);
    }
    return playerData;
}
console.log(playerWithAges(players, playerAges));
```

```
TERMINAL   PROBLEMS   OUTPUT   DEBUG CONSOLE                                    1: bash            ⌄

yueha@DESKTOP-MBVNIFF MINGW64 ~/repos/js-coding-for-teens/exercises/ch7 (master)
$ node playerAges.js
[
  { name: 'superb', skill: 3, age: 21 },
  { name: 'smirk', skill: 7, age: 21 },
  { name: 'tired', skill: 6, age: 22 },
  { name: 'ANS', skill: 9, age: 21 }
]
```

Very nice! If any part of this question left you scratching your head, write a table.

Crack the Code

With this chapter, you have finally covered the core fundamentals of programming. But you aren't done. In fact, this is just the start!

1. After this code is run, is **players** an array with **"smurf"** and **"ANS"** in it? Why or why not?

   ```
   var players = ['super', 'smurf', 'ANS'];
   players = players.shift();
   players;
   ```

2. What is mutability? What data types are mutable?

3. Why does string modification require a reassignment, while array and object modification do not?

4. What array methods decrease the size of an array?

5. What array methods increase the size of the array?

6. Draw a table for the following function. Write what the **array** will look like on each iteration and **array.length > 0**.

   ```
   function destroyArray(array) {
       var i = 0;
       while (array.length > 0) {
           array.pop();
           i++;
       }
   }
   var arr = [10, 20, 12, 30, 25];
   destroyArray(arr);
   ```

7. What is the output of the following code? Draw a table if necessary.

   ```
   function modifyString(str) {
       var newStr = '';
   ```

```
        for (var i = 0; i < str.length - 1; i++) {
            newStr += str[i];
        }
        return newStr;
    }
    modifyString('abcdefg')
```

8. In your own words, describe what the purpose of this function is. Why does it work for both strings and arrays? Draw a table for each sample function invocation.

```
    function mysteryFunc(arrOrStr, item) {
        for (var i = 0; i < arrOrStr.length; i++) {
            var currItem = arrOrStr[i];
            if (currItem === item) {
                return true;
            }
        }
        return false;
    }
    mysteryFunc('cat', 'a'); // true
    mysteryFunc('cat', 'b'); // false
    mysteryFunc([30, 11], 1); // false
    mysteryFunc([30, 11], 11); // true
```

9. What is the value of count?

```
    var count = 0;
    function increment() {
        count += 1;
    }
    increment();
    increment();
    console.log(count);
```

Debugging

This code has a ton of problems! The function **playerAboveSkillAndAge** should be returning an array that includes the players who are above the specified skill and age.

```
    var players = [
        { player: 'super', skill: 1, age: 20 },
        { player: 'smurf', skill: 8, age: 24 },
```

```javascript
    { player: 'ANS', skill: 6, age: 27 },
    { player: 'faker', skill: 10, age: 17 },
    { player: 'shroud', skill: 9, age: 26 }
];
function playersAboveSkill(players, skill) {
    var skilledPlayers = players;
    for (var i = 0; i < players.length; i++) {
        var objectKey = 'skill';
        if (players[i].objectKey < skill) {
            skilledPlayers.push(players);
        }
    }
    return skilledPlayers;
}
function playersAboveAge(players, age) {
    var agedPlayers = players;
    for (var i = 1; i < players.length; i++) {
        var objectKey = 'age';
        if (players[i].objectKey < age) {
            agedPlayers.push(players);
        }
    }
    return agedPlayers;
}
function playerAboveSkillAndAge(players, skill, age) {
    var skilledPlayers = playersAboveSkill(players, skill);
    var skilledAndAgedPlayers = playersAboveAge(skilledPlayers, age);
    return skilledAndAgedPlayers;
}
console.log(playerAboveSkillAndAge(players, 6, 19));
// expected
[
    { player: 'smurf', skill: 8, age: 24 },
    { player: 'shroud', skill: 9, age: 26 }
];
console.log(playerAboveSkillAndAge(players, 2, 16));
// expected
[
```

```
    { player: 'smurf', skill: 8, age: 24 },
    { player: 'ANS', skill: 6, age: 27 },
    { player: 'faker', skill: 10, age: 17 },
    { player: 'shroud', skill: 9, age: 26 }
];
```

CODER'S CHECKLIST » Let's review the topics we covered

You've come a long way! You are now officially done with programming fundamentals. Moving forward, you are going to learn about features that are more specific to JavaScript. That means object-oriented programming and website programming. The challenges are going to get harder, but you've been slowly building yourself up to make sure you're prepared to face them.

- ☐ Adding and removing elements from an array
- ☐ Converting a string of numbers into the number data type
- ☐ Accessing characters in a string by index
- ☐ Adding and updating keys in an object

CHAPTER 8

Object-Oriented Programming

So far, we have discussed that an object is a data structure that holds key-value pairs. It is also important to know that the word "object" has multiple meanings in JavaScript. The objects that will be discussed are a core design principle that JavaScript is built on. In this chapter, you'll be making your own and applying them in challenges where their utility shines!

Objects as Entities

There is a type of data in JavaScript that is called an "object" but is *not* a data structure. It is an entity—a collection of functions and properties wrapped up in a tidy package. Let's look at a few examples to learn more about objects.

DOGS AS REAL-WORLD OBJECTS

Let's describe a dog in a technical fashion. They have many qualifiable aspects about them, such as age, name, sex, and fur color. Dogs are also capable of performing actions, such as running, barking, and eating.

DOGS AS INDIVIDUALS

What about a specific dog? My neighbor has a dog whose name is Sparky. My favorite part about Sparky is the fact that he barks very loudly at 6:00 a.m. I love waking up to Sparky's barking, because I don't like getting eight hours of quality sleep each night. There are many dogs who share all of the same properties, but there is only one Sparky, the special dog in my neighborhood who likes to remind me that sleeping is a bad idea.

Sparky is the only dog in the world who is Sparky. So, they are their own entity. In JavaScript, Sparky would be referred to as an **object instance**.

```
var sparky = new Dog();
```

Dogs as JavaScript Objects

The ideas that were just presented have the same parallels in programming. A dog object would have many **properties** about itself and have many **methods** that it could invoke.

OBJECT PROPERTY

In JavaScript, to access the **age** of the dog, it looks like this.

```
sparky.age; // 10
```

OBJECT METHOD

If Sparky wants to bark, a method called **bark** would be invoked.

```
sparky.bark(); // 'ruff ruff!'
```

Notice how bark looks similar to a function call? That's because **methods** are actually functions! Methods are functions that are specific to an object instance. They can't be used on anything else.

JavaScript Object Implementation

In order to leverage the power of objects, we have to learn the full JavaScript syntax to write them.

CONSTRUCTOR FUNCTION

In JavaScript, functions are dual-purpose. They can be used as normal functions to invoke code, which you have already learned, and they can be used as a **constructor function**. A **constructor** is a function that is called to create an object instance.

This is where **pascal case,** with the first letter of every word capitalized, is the accepted **convention**.

```
function Dog() {
}
```

For object instances, the keyword **new** is needed in front of the function invocation.

```
var sparky = new Dog();
```

OBJECT PROPERTY

Adding an object property is essentially the same as adding a key-value pair. Except it is done in a constructor function.

```
function Dog() {
    this.age = 10;
}
var sparky = new Dog();
sparky.age; // 10
```

Wait! What is this variable, **this**? Well, it is a secret variable that is automatically created by a `function`. It has some important properties when it comes to object-oriented programming. Most important, **this** can be assigned key-value pairs.

OBJECT METHODS

In JavaScript, functions also have a secret property named **prototype**. Its duty is to store methods that the function will have available to the object instance. To create methods, the function expression syntax is required.

```
function Dog() {
}
Dog.prototype.bark = function() {
    console.log('ruff ruff!');
};
var sparky = new Dog();
sparky.bark(); // 'ruff ruff!'
```

INSTANCE VARIABLE

Now that you have knowledge of the basic syntax, we should talk about the secret variable **this**. It is available in a constructor function. Key-value pairs can be added to **this**. The key-value pairs that are added to this are commonly referred to as **instance variables**.

```
function Dog() {
    this.name = 'sparky';
}
Dog.prototype.speak = function() {
    console.log('ruff ruff, my name is' + this.name);
};
var sparky = new Dog();
sparky.speak(); // 'ruff ruff, my name is sparky'
```

TERMINAL   PROBLEMS   OUTPUT   DEBUG CONSOLE   1: bash   ∨

yueha@DESKTOP-MBVNIFF MINGW64 ~/repos/js-coding-for-teens/exercises/ch8 (master)
$ node speak.js
ruff ruff, my name is sparky

For now, ignore the fact that this dog can speak English. You are more interested in the fact that **this.name**, created in the constructor, is magically available in a method. This is extremely important to remember: Any method that has been assigned to **Dog.prototype** has the variable **this** available to it.

INSTANCE VARIABLE MODIFICATION

Since **this** is available in every method, instance variables can be modified in methods as well.

```
function Dog() {
    this.name = 'sparky';
    this.age = 0
}
Dog.prototype.growOlder = function() {
    this.age += 1
};
var sparky = new Dog();
sparky.age // 0
sparky.growOlder();
sparky.age // 1
```

HACKER HINT

Instance variables can be created in methods as well, but it is not encouraged. In a majority of situations, there are better ways the code could be written.

Object-Oriented Programming in Action

Seeing is believing, so build your understanding of object-oriented programming with a JavaScript **Dog** whose abilities will match real-life dogs.

DOG PROPERTIES

In order to make an object instance, a constructor function is required.

```
function Dog() {
}
var sparky = new Dog();
```

This is pretty boring and doesn't tell you much about dogs. There are so many aspects of dogs that you likely want your object to know about. This can be done by making them instance variables. A dog's **name**, **age**, **weight**, and **legCount** can be stored. A typical dog has 4 legs. But **name**, **age**, and **weight** vary among dogs. Add them as parameters in our constructor function.

```
function Dog(name, age, weight) {
}
```

In order to track data in each **Dog** instance, add these values as key-value pairs to **this**.

```
function Dog(name, age, weight) {
    this.name = name;
    this.age = age;
    this.weight = weight;
    this.legCount = 4;
}
var sparky = new Dog('sparky', 4, 20);
var misu = new Dog('misu', 10, 15);
sparky.name; // 'sparky'
sparky.weight; // '20'
misu.name; // 'misu'
misu.weight; // 15
```

Great! Now that you understand how to use constructor functions to create object instances, you have two independent dogs with their respective **names**, **ages**, and **weights**.

DOG METHODS

Currently, these dogs don't know how to do anything. To change that, add a few methods.

First, dogs should be able to eat food. Add an **eat** method.

```
Dog.prototype.eat = function() {
    console.log('nom nom nom');
};
var sparky = new Dog('sparky', 4, 20);
sparky.eat(); // 'nom nom nom'
```

When a dog eats too much, it will gain weight. A method can be written to represent this. Just like with any function, methods can accept parameters.

Then, add a parameter that represents the amount of weight gained from overeating.

```
Dog.prototype.eatTooMuch = function(weightGain) {
    console.log('ugh... ' + this.name + ' doesn\'t feel so good');
    this.weight += weightGain;
};
var sparky = new Dog('sparky', 4, 20);
sparky.weight; // 20
sparky.eatTooMuch(2); // 'ugh ... sparky doesn't feel so good'
sparky.weight; // 22
```

It's important to remember that **this** is available to us in all methods that are assigned to our constructor function, **Dog**. The **eatTooMuch** method is able to modify the dog's **weight**.

Methods are functions with modified syntax. You have used functions extensively for calculations. You can do the same again here. Make a method that computes a dog's age in dog years, like **ageInDogYears** method. The rule of thumb to equate a human age to a dog's is to multiply by seven.

```
Dog.prototype.ageInDogYears = function(weightGain) {
    return this.age * 7;
};
var sparky = new Dog('sparky', 4, 20);
sparky.ageInDogYears(); // 28
```

But wait! Sparky has decided to be greedy and is now stealing food from a feline friend. In a new **stealCatFood** method, you can express the facts that Sparky has consumed food and is being mischievous in the process.

HACKER HINT

Creating a method is a straightforward way of breaking up a complex method. It is encouraged to make new, smaller methods, even if the method itself is not used anywhere else or by any object instances.

Methods can be called inside other methods. An **eat** method has already been created, so you can reuse it. In order to express the mischievous nature of the canine, an extra **console.log** message can also be shown.

```
Dog.prototype.eat = function() {
    console.log('nom nom nom');
};
```

```
Dog.prototype.stealCatFood = function() {
    this.eat();
    console.log('Yuck, cat food is gross!');
};
var sparky = new Dog('sparky', 4, 20);
sparky.stealCatFood();
// 'nom nom nom'
// 'Yuck, cat food is gross!'
```

When calling a method inside another method, **prototype** is never referenced. It is `this.eat`. Not `this.prototype.eat`.

Crack the Code

As the complexity of the programming tools and principles increases, it gets harder to mentally keep track of everything. You have reached a point where online resources are your best friend! Don't be shy about going online to discover more insight on the topics covered in this chapter. Some suggested resources are listed in the back of this book.

1. Define what an object data structure is.
2. Define what an object is in object-oriented programming.
3. What variable is available across all methods?
4. What is the syntax to invoke a method inside another method?
5. What is the syntax to make a constructor?
6. What is an object instance?
7. What is the syntax to initialize an object instance?

Debugging

A rudimentary chat program is having problems running correctly. The method **printLog** should print the chat history. This one is a little tricky, because two objects are interacting with each other. You're using data structures in an advanced way, so don't be shy about using `console.log` to check the values of variables.

```
function Person(name) {
    this.name = name;
}
function ChatProgram() {
    this.chatLog = [];
}
ChatProgram.prototype.message = function (person, message) {
    var messageEntry = {
```

```
            person: person,
            message: message
        };
        this.chatLog(messageEntry);
    };
    ChatProgram.prototype.parseMessageEntry = function (chatEntry) {
        return chatEntry.person.name + ': ' + chatEntry.chat;
    };
    ChatProgram.prototype.getLog = function () {
        var allMessages = [];
        for (var i = 0; i < this.chatLog.length; i++) {
            var chatEntry = this.chatLog[i];
            var parsedMessage = this.prototype.parseMessageEntry(chatEntry);
            allMessages.pop(parsedMessage);
        }
        return allMessages;
    };
    ChatProgram.prototype.printLog = function () {
        var allMessages = this.getLog;
        for (var i = 0; i < allMessages.length; i++) {
            console.log(allMessages[i]);
        }
    };
    var layna = new Person('Layna');
    var andrew = new Person('Andrew');
    var chat = new ChatProgram();
    chat.message(andrew, 'Hi Layna, how\'s it going?');
    chat.message(layna, 'I\'m doing great');
    chat.message(layna, 'What about you?');
    chat.message(andrew, 'I just came back from the doctor');
    chat.message(layna, 'Wow, this conversation is really boring');
    chat.message(andrew, 'That was really mean, why would you say some-
    thing like that?');
    chat.message(layna, 'I have better things to do');
    chat.message(andrew, ':(');
    chat.message(layna, 'Goodbye');
    chat.printLog();
```

This is the expected output.

```
TERMINAL   PROBLEMS   OUTPUT   DEBUG CONSOLE                              1: bash          ⌄

yueha@DESKTOP-MBVNIFF MINGW64 ~/repos/js-coding-for-teens/Chapters/8-OOP (master)
$ node debugging.js
Andrew: Hi Layna, how's it going?
Layna: I'm doing great
Layna: What about you?
Andrew: I just came back from the doctor
Layna: Wow, this conversation is really boring
Andrew: That was really mean, why would you say something like that?
Layna: I have better things to do
Andrew: :(
Layna: Goodbye
```

CODER'S CHECKLIST » Let's review the topics we covered

Object-oriented programming isn't unique to JavaScript, but it is the first topic that is
not universal among all programming languages. Object-oriented programming is one
strategy, out of many, for solving a programming challenge. As you accumulate more
techniques in your programming tool kit, you will find multiple approaches to solving
a problem. It takes experience and intuition to discover the best way to solve it. If you
have an idea that you're unsure of, give it a shot anyway! Programming is all about
learning from past mistakes. Here's a quick review of what you learned in this chapter.

☐ What an object is   ☐ What an object   ☐ How to create   ☐ How to create
                           instance is   instance variables   methods

CHAPTER 9

JavaScript and the Web

Everything that (boring) HTML can do can be done using JavaScript—and then some! To prove it, in this chapter, you'll start with HTML on a web page, show how the same thing can be done in JavaScript, and then take it a step beyond what HTML can do. This is your first taste of what modern JavaScript is and where it shines. I hope you're as excited as I am!

Abstraction Level of the Web

Websites are on an entirely different level of abstraction when compared to your standard terminal. If the abstraction level of `console.log` is like riding a bike, JavaScript and its web development features are like driving a car.

For this chapter, you are not concerned with how the tools work. You are only concerned with your ability to leverage the tools to perform meaningful tasks on the web browser.

HTML: HyperText Markup Language

You will lean very heavily on JavaScript, but a small amount of hypertext markup language, or **HTML**, is still required to interact with a web page. Modern websites use incredible amounts of JavaScript to manipulate it.

HTML FILE

In the same way JavaScript has its own file extension, .js, HTML has its own file extension, .html. Make an HTML file. This is the bare minimum for something to be considered a web page. I have named mine index.html, which is the standard name for the first HTML file.

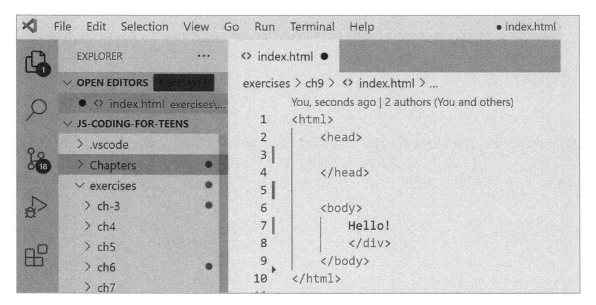

HTML TAG

Notice the angle brackets surrounding a word? That is HTML syntax.

```
<valid-html-tag-name-here>
```

One has angle brackets surrounding it and one has an angle bracket and a slash. The angle bracket-only tag is referred to as the **open tag** and the other, with the slash, is the **close tag**. An open tag must have a correlating close tag.

```
<html>
</html>
```

Any amount of content can be placed between the open and close tags. HTML can get incredibly complex!

HTML TAGS WE WILL USE

Because the emphasis of this book is on JavaScript, there will be only a handful of HTML tags covered.

```
<html>
    <head>
```

```
    </head>
    <body>
        <div>
            Hello!
        </div>
    </body>
</html>
```

The `html` tag is the main tag that wraps around all HTML in a file. The head tag is multi-purpose. It is usually the place where nonvisual HTML is inserted. The **body** tag is where visual elements are placed. **div** is a tag that doesn't have an important role. It is simply used to wrap elements inside it.

HTML ATTRIBUTES: CLASS AND ID

There are many different **HTML attributes**. The syntax to apply them is the attribute name, an equal sign, and the value (double quotes). As a concept, it is quite similar to a key-value pair in an object data structure.

```
<div class="container">
    I am content in a div!
</div>
```

The attributes **class** and **id** are important to have in HTML. The go-to strategy, when working with JavaScript, is to find HTML elements by their `class` or `id`.

Web Browser

Before starting, make sure the web browser Google Chrome is installed. Not all browsers are built the same and Google Chrome is very good at running JavaScript.

Search engine query: "google chrome download"
Current URL: **google.com/chrome**

WEB BROWSER DEVELOPER TOOLS

After installation, open Google Chrome. Navigate to Settings (the triple dot at the top right) -> More Tools -> Developer Tools.

The **developer console** will appear. As a JavaScript programmer, this is where all of the magic happens. JavaScript can be written inside. It is almost like a mini terminal built into the browser.

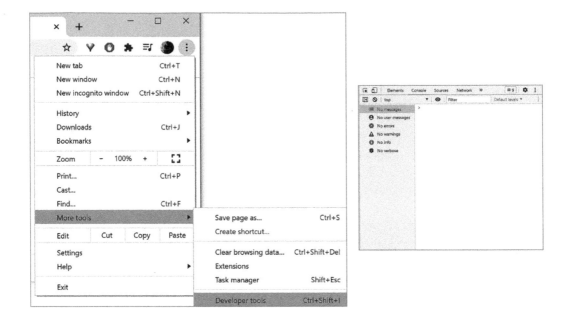

Remember the barebones index.html (page 104)? Find the file in your operating system's (PC or Mac) file system. The easiest way to find it is to right click the file in VS Code and select "Reveal in File Explorer." For Macs, it is "Reveal in Finder." Code will open the directory where the file exists.

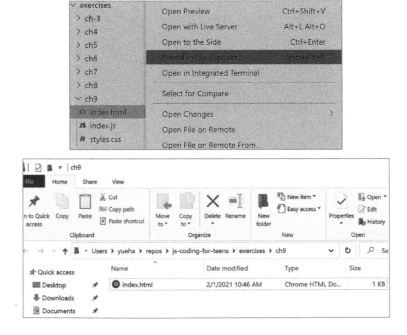

If the file already has the Google Chrome icon, double click the file to open it. The file can also be dragged and dropped to the browser window.

Notice how the location is not an internet URL? That's the directory path to the HTML file. After confirming the file is running, modify the HTML.

```
<html>
    <head>
    </head>
    <body>
        <div>
            Hello!
        </div>
        <div>
            I am EXTREMELY cool
        </div>
    </body>
</html>
```

After modification, the page has not changed. Why isn't the browser acknowledging the fact that we are extremely cool? That's because the browser has the old version of the file loaded. In order to see updates, refresh the page.

After a refresh, we see our update. Very nice!

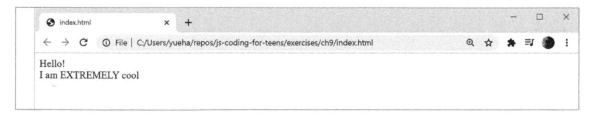

Document

In the browser, there is a variable that is automatically created called **document**. Type it into the developer console. The variable is a JavaScript object that refers to the entire page. After expansion, all the HTML is revealed. Use your mouse cursor and hover over the document variable. Notice how the web page is blue?

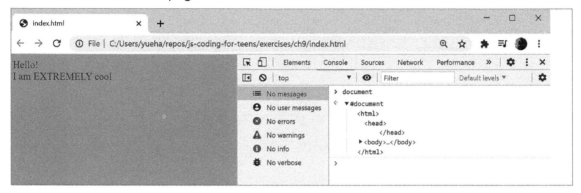

The developer console highlights HTML that the cursor is hovering over. To further prove this, expand the **body** and hover over a highlighted **div** element.

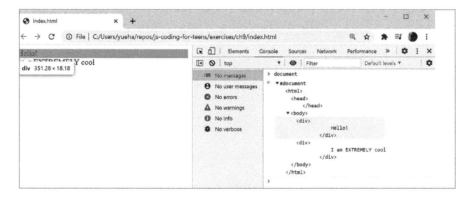

HTML Selectors

JavaScript has many browser-related functions to use. **document** is an object, which means it has methods. The available methods can modify HTML. The entire web development community relies heavily on this handful of methods and functions.

DOCUMENT.GETELEMENTSBYCLASSNAME

One method on the **document** object that will be used extensively is **document.get ElementsByClassName**. If we change the div HTML elements to have class attributes, **document.getElementsByClassName** can work its magic!

```
<html>
    <head>
    </head>
    <body>
        <div class="cool-message">
            Hello!
        </div>
        <div class="cool-message">
            I am EXTREMELY cool
        </div>
    </body>
</html>
```

document.getElementsByClassName accepts one parameter. It is the string name of the class. The **class "cool-message"** was added to the **div** elements. This attribute will be used to identify the HTML elements. Use the following code in the developer console. After the code is run, type the variable name to show its value in the console.

```
var divElements = document.getElementsByClassName('cool-message');
```

After the code is run, type the variable name **divElements** into the console again to show its value.

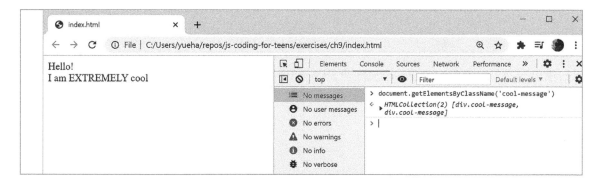

Great! Looks like the statement returned an array of our two HTML elements! Well, technically, it is a data structure called an **HTMLCollection**. Moving forward, HTMLCollections will be referred to as an **array-like data structure**. But don't worry, because the distinction between arrays and array-like data structures won't impact you. Loops work on HTMLCollections.

DOCUMENT.GETELEMENTBYID

In the same way **document.getElementsByClassName** gets HTML elements by their **class** attribute, **document.getElementById** selects an element by its **id** attribute. In order to have an element get selected by **document.getElementById**, modify the HTML. Add a **div** element with an **id** attribute.

```
<html>
    <head>
    </head>
    <body>
        <div class="cool-message">
            Hello!
        </div>
        <div class="cool-message">
            I am EXTREMELY cool
        </div>
        <div id="occupation">
            That is because I am a programmer
        </div>
    </body>
</html>
```

Refresh the page. Type the following code into the developer console. After typing the variable name into the console again, the return value should be pointing to the third line of text.

```
var divElement = document.getElementById('occupation');
```

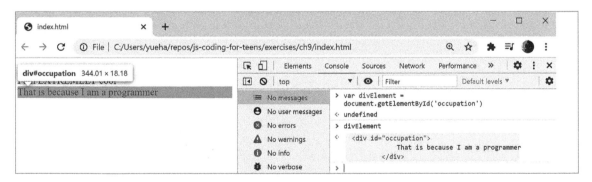

Notice how **document.getElementById** returns a single element? It does not return an array-like data structure, like **document.getElementsByClassName** does. That's because **document.getElementById** can only select one element at a time.

HTML Manipulation

HTML elements have many methods and properties in them, just like the **document** object. These methods and properties give us the ability to modify specific HTML elements.

ACCESS TEXT WITH INNERHTML

When writing text on the page and wrapping it inside HTML, **div** is the most straightforward tag to use. When JavaScript uses a selector to point to the HTML, it is represented as a JavaScript object. This object has a key named **innerHTML**. It holds the text inside an HTML element. This can be seen by revisiting your sample HTML. Grab the text inside the **div** with the **id** of **"occupation"** using **document.getElementById**.

```html
<html>
    <head>
    </head>
    <body>
        <div class="cool-message">
            Hello!
        </div>
        <div class="cool-message">
            I am EXTREMELY cool
        </div>
        <div id="occupation">
            That is because I am a programmer
        </div>
    </body>
</html>
```

```js
var divElement = document.getElementById('occupation');
divElement.innerHTML;
```

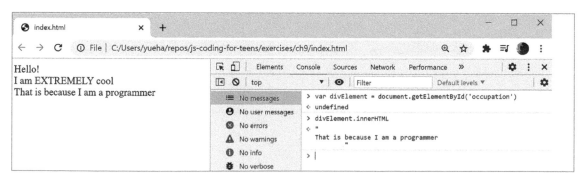

INJECTING NEW TEXT WITH INNERHTML

innerHTML is a property on the object. Just like with any key-value pair on an object, it can be reassigned. This allows modification of the text inside.

```
var divElement = document.getElementById('occupation');
divElement.innerHTML += ' and love building things';
```

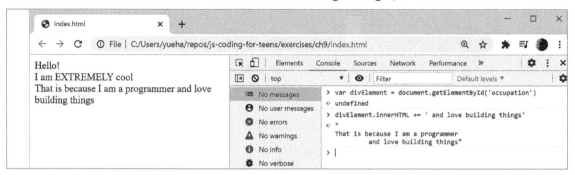

Using the self-addition operator, extra text was appended to the **div** element's **innerHTML**. Congrats! You have taken the first step into the world of web development.

UPDATING ATTRIBUTE ID

In the same way **innerHTML** can be updated, the attributes **class** and **id** can be changed as well. Updating the **id** of an HTML element is easy. The key is **id**.

```
var divElement = document.getElementById('occupation');
divElement.id = 'new-id';
```

UPDATING ATTRIBUTE CLASS

Updating **class** is trickier than **id**. This is because it is common to have multiple classes assigned. Revisit the HTML file. Right now, the **div** elements have a single **class**.

```
<html>
    <head>
    </head>
    <body>
        <div class="cool-message">
            Hello!
        </div>
        <div class="cool-message">
            I am EXTREMELY cool
        </div>
```

```html
        <div id="occupation">
            That is because I am a programmer
        </div>
    </body>
</html>
```

The method to add a class to an existing HTML element is **classList.add**. It takes a single parameter, which is the name of the **class**, to append.

```javascript
var divElements = document.getElementsByClassName('cool-message');
divElements[0].classList.add('new-class');
```

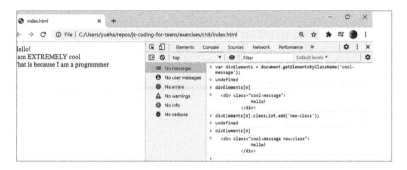

The method to remove a class is **classList.remove**, which takes a single argument that is the name of the **class** to be removed.

```javascript
var divElements = document.getElementsByClassName('cool-message');
divElements[0].classList.remove('new-class');
```

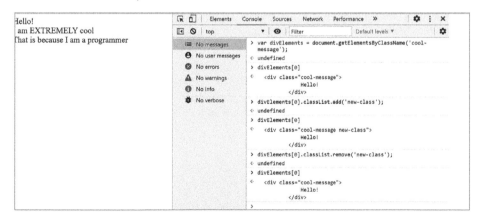

PURPOSE OF CHANGING HTML CLASS

So far, you've been doing a lot of work to learn about how to change an HTML element's `class`. This becomes important when you're working with CSS. This book won't be covering CSS, but just know that updating the `class` attribute is a common way of triggering visual changes on HTML elements.

Creating HTML Elements

The **document** object also has methods to create HTML elements. This will become especially important when you make your game!

DOCUMENT.CREATEELEMENT

Using **document.createElement**, JavaScript can create HTML. It accepts one parameter, which is the string name of the HTML tag. Because we aren't learning much HTML, we will always be creating a `div` element when using **document.createElement**.

```
var div = document.createElement('div');
div.innerHTML = 'I am a new div!';
```

An HTML `div` has been created with **innerHTML**: "I am a new div!" But where is it? It isn't on the page. You've created it, but you haven't put it anywhere!

APPENDING HTML TO THE PAGE

An HTML element that is created with JavaScript needs to be manually added to the page. This is where the method **append** is used. It exists on the HTML object that is retrieved using any HTML selector, such as **document.getElementsByClassName** and **document.getElementById**.

```
var div = document.createElement('div');
div.innerHTML = 'I am a new div!';
var divElements = document.getElementsByClassName('cool-message');
divElements.append(div);
```

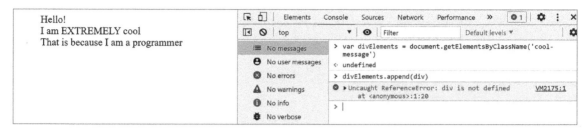

Whoops! Why did this not work? That's because **document.getElementsByClassName** returns an array-like data structure.

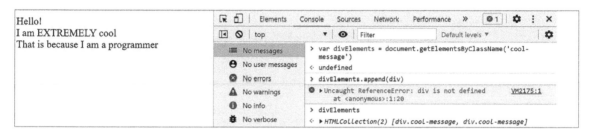

Accessing an element in the array-like data structure can be done by index.

```
var div = document.createElement('div');
div.innerHTML = 'I am a new div!';
var divElements = document.getElementsByClassName('cool-message');
divElements[1].append(div);
```

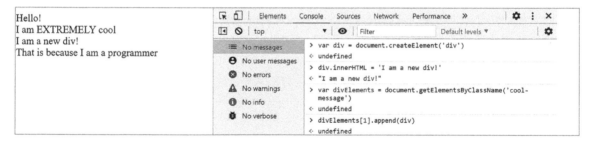

You just used pure JavaScript to make HTML! I think that's pretty cool.

REMOVING HTML FROM THE PAGE

JavaScript can be used to remove HTML elements as well. Modify the HTML file with a new **div** element that has an **id** attribute with some **innerHTML**.

```
<html>
    <head>
    </head>
```

```
<body>
    <div class="cool-message">
        Hello!
    </div>
    <div class="cool-message">
        I am EXTREMELY cool
    </div>
    <div id="occupation">
        That is because I am a programmer
    </div>
    <div id="untrue-message">
        Just kidding, programmers are losers
    </div>
</body>
</html>
```

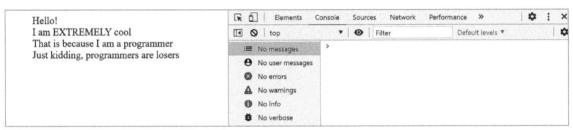

Programmers are losers? Seeing this false statement makes my blood boil. I demand that **div** be removed from the page. That statement's **div** has an **id**. That means **document. getElementById** can be used to point to that HTML element.

```
var slanderousDiv = document.getElementById('untrue-message');
```

The method to operate on the **slanderousDiv** variable is **remove**, which has no parameters.

```
var slanderousDiv = document.getElementById('untrue-message');
slanderousDiv.remove();
```

Excellent! The **div**, along with the content inside of it, has been destroyed with extreme prejudice.

Running JavaScript in HTML

So far, updates on the page have been done in the developer console. But, clearly, that is not how programmers build websites! In order to run thousands of lines of code, programmers need to be able to write JavaScript into the file and have the code run automatically.

HTML SCRIPT TAG

The HTML **script** tag allows you to place JavaScript code inside an HTML file. The code within the open and closing tags will automatically run when the page loads. For the most consistent results, place the **script** under the **body** tag.

```
<html>
    <head>
    </head>
    <body>
        <div class="cool-message">
            Hello!
        </div>
        <div class="cool-message">
            I am EXTREMELY cool
        </div>
        <div id="occupation">
            That is because I am a programmer
        </div>
    </body>
    <script>
        console.log('Hi! I have been automatically invoked in the browser')
    </script>
</html>
```

Refresh the page. You will see that with the JavaScript code wrapped in the **script** tag, the code **console.log** has been automatically invoked.

The ability to put JavaScript in an HTML file empowers programmers to create dynamic websites. The browser truly is the place where JavaScript shines!

Mass Updating HTML

With an understanding of how to run code when the page loads, you are ready to write meaningful code. First, remove all of the visual content in the HTML file. Only leave an empty `div` that has an `id`.

```
<html>
    <head>
    </head>
    <body>
        <div id="container">
        </div>
    </body>
    <script>

    </script>
</html>
```

Inside the `script` tag, you can use your understanding of data structures, loops, and HTML manipulation to recreate the content you were originally hard coding. The first step is to make a function that will create `div` elements with `innerHTML` text content.

```
function createDivWithText(text) {
    var div = document.createElement('div');
    div.innerHTML = text;
    return div;
}
```

Next, an array of text to add to the page.

```
var htmlText = ['Hello!', 'I am EXTREMELY cool', 'That is because
I am a programmer'];
```

At this point, there is a function that creates HTML and an array of text. Sounds like you need a for loop, doesn't it?

```
for (var i = 0; i < htmlText.length; i++) {
    var newDiv = createDivWithText(htmlText[i]);
}
```

But what do you do with this **newDiv**? You need a place to insert it! That's where `document.getElementById` is used.

Remember the empty `div` with the `id` "container"? Point to the `div` with JavaScript and then **append** the newly created `div` elements, one by one.

```
function createDivWithText(text) {
    var div = document.createElement('div');
    div.innerHTML = text;
    return div;
}
var htmlText = ['Hello!', 'I am EXTREMELY cool', 'That is because
I am a programmer'];
var container = document.getElementById('container');
for (var i = 0; i < htmlText.length; i++) {
    var newDiv = createDivWithText(htmlText[i]);
    container.append(newDiv);
}
```
Putting it all together, the HTML file looks like this:
```
<html>
    <head>
    </head>
    <body>
        <div id="container">
        </div>
    </body>
    <script>
        function createDivWithText(text) {
            var div = document.createElement('div');
            div.innerHTML = text;
            return div;
        }
        var htmlText = ['Hello!', 'I am EXTREMELY cool', 'That is because
        I am a programmer'];
        var container = document.getElementById('container');
        for (var i = 0; i < htmlText.length; i++) {
            var newDiv = createDivWithText(htmlText[i]);
            container.append(newDiv);
        }
    </script>
</html>
```
After refreshing the page, the HTML is all there. JavaScript was used to create the same content!

script Tag Importing

Adding JavaScript code inside an HTML file works well for a few hundred lines. But professional programs run massive amounts of code. Because of this, it is preferable to separate the HTML file from the JavaScript that it runs.

To do this, place the code that was written in a new JavaScript file. The traditional file name is index.js. Keep in mind that it is much easier to keep track of files when they are in the same directory.

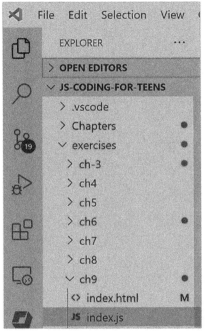
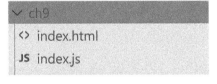

```
// index.js
function createDivWithText(text) {
    var div = document.createElement('div');
    div.innerHTML = text;
    return div;
}
var htmlText = ['Hello!', 'I am EXTREMELY cool', 'That is because I am a
programmer'];
var container = document.getElementById('container');
for (var i = 0; i < htmlText.length; i++) {
    var newDiv = createDivWithText(htmlText[i]);
    container.append(newDiv);
```

```
}
```

Now that the JavaScript code is transferred to a .js file, the HTML file is quite empty.

```html
<html>
    <head>
    </head>
    <body>
        <div id="container">
        </div>
    </body>
</html>
```

But how does the index.html file know where to find the JavaScript code? The **script** tag can be used again. But instead of writing the code inside, use the **src** attribute to point to the JavaScript file! Because our files exist in the same directory, directory paths don't need to be accounted for. Just write the file name as the value.

```html
<html>
    <head>
    </head>
    <body>
        <div id="container">
        </div>
    </body>
    <script src="index.js"></script>
</html>
```

Upon refresh, the page is identical. You have successfully separated the HTML file and the JavaScript code that it runs!

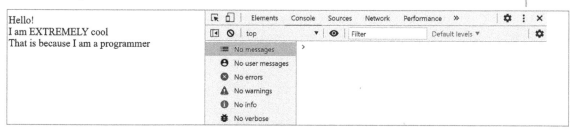

JavaScript Event Listeners

Clicking a button on a modern website can create a range of effects, from a small pop-up window to a visual rehaul of the entire page. JavaScript has the incredible power to respond to user actions. It does this through the use of **event listeners**. Event listeners can be either appended to the entire document object or to individual HTML elements.

JavaScript can listen and invoke behavior to things such as:

→ Mouse hovering over HTML elements

→ Clicks on a button

→ Keypresses on the keyboard

To start your exploration of event listeners, add a **button** to an empty page. Clear out the index.js file as well.

```html
<html>
    <head>
    </head>
    <body>
        <button id="clickable-button">
            Click me!
        </button>
    </body>
    <script src="index.js"></script>
</html>
```

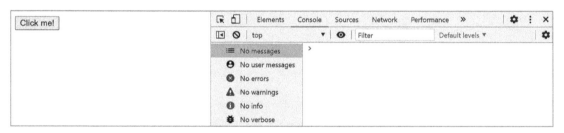

Clicking on the button that says "Click me!" does . . . nothing? HTML can be used to create actions on click, but we are more interested in how JavaScript can do it.

A method that exists on all HTML elements is called **addEventListener**. It takes two arguments. The first is the name of the event to watch for and the second is a **function** that will be triggered when that particular event occurs. Inside the function, place an **alert** to confirm that the event listener works.

```javascript
// index.js
var button = document.getElementById('clickable-button');
button.addEventListener('click', function () {
    alert('I have been clicked!');
});
```

You are looking for a mouse click. Don't sweat the details on the second parameter and how it works. Just know that it needs to be a function.

On refresh, clicking the **button** will result in a pop-up alert, just as expected.

The click event is one of many types of events available in JavaScript. If you want to know more about which ones are available, there are online resources to find them.

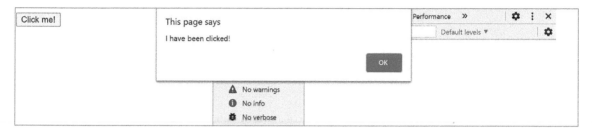

The method **addEventListener**'s second parameter, which is a function, has its own parameter. It is commonly referred to as the **event object**. To see what it looks like, use **console.log** inside the function.

```
// index.js
var button = document.getElementById( 'clickable-button');
button.addEventListener('click', function (event) {
    console.log(event);
});
```

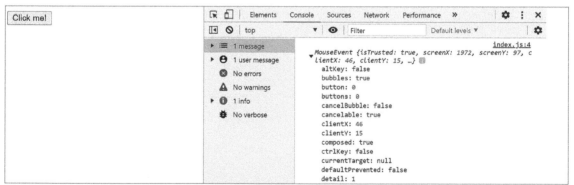

Wow, that is a lot of information! Don't worry about the information that exists in the **event**. For now, just know that **addEventListener** provides information about the click event.

Hiding Elements Using CSS

CSS works very well in conjunction with JavaScript. There are two different ways of creating elements on the page. One is to manually create them and the other is to reveal hidden elements.

APPLYING CSS TO HTML

There are two different ways to apply CSS styling onto a page. One is using the **style** tag. CSS can be wrapped inside and styles will be applied via the attribute **class**. Here, the class name **hide** is being added to your button with correlating CSS to make the **button** invisible.

```
<html>
    <head>
        <style>
            .hide {
                opacity: 0;
            }
        </style>
    </head>
    <body>
        <button id="clickable-button" class="hide">
            Click me!
        </button>
    </body>
    <script src="index.js"></script>
</html>
```

Inspecting this on the browser, the **button** is now gone! But if you inspect the page, the **button** is still there! It is just invisible.

The other method is importing a CSS file, which is more commonly used. This is done using the **link** tag and giving the tag **rel** and **href** attributes. The **rel** value is always **"stylesheets"** and the **href** is the file name. Let's modify it so the styles are in a separate file but still applied to the page.

Make a new file with the CSS extension, .css. Mine will be named styles.css.

```css
.hide {
    opacity: 0;
}
```

Then import it using the **link** tag. Nothing should change!

```html
<html>
    <head>
        <link rel="stylesheet" href="styles.css">
    </head>
    <body>
        <button id="clickable-button" class="hide">
            Click me!
        </button>
    </body>
    <script src="index.js"></script>
</html>
```

SHOWING AND HIDING ELEMENTS USING CSS

CSS can be applied to hide elements and JavaScript can manipulate HTML, including classes and ids. This means you can show and hide elements using code! Let's do just that. Add an HTML element with the class **hide** and an id so **getElementById** can be used.

```html
<html>
    <head>
        <link rel="stylesheet" href="styles.css">
    </head>
    <body>
        <button id="clickable-button">
            Click me!
        </button>
        <div class="hide" id="content">
            Content!
        </div>
    </body>
    <script src="index.js"></script>
</html>
```

Then, in the JavaScript file, add behavior to the button event listener to remove the class from the HTML element.

```
// index.js
var button = document.getElementById('clickable-button');
button.addEventListener('click', function () {
    var hiddenElement = document.getElementById('content');
    hiddenElement.classList.remove('hide');
});
```
After clicking the button, the hidden content should be revealed.

```
Click me!
Content!

⚫ ▢ | Elements  Console  Sources  Network  Performance  »    ⚙ ⋮ ✕
<html>
  ▶ <head>...</head>
···▼<body> == $0
        <button id="clickable-button">
                Click me!
        </button>
        <div class id="content">
                Content!
        </div>
        <script src="index.js"></script>
      </body>
</html>
```

Browser-Specific JavaScript in Action

Now that you have a general understanding of how JavaScript interacts with the browser and HTML, it's time to step up your game for a bigger challenge!

TYPE ON THE PAGE

For this exercise, you will make your website detect keystrokes and put it on the page! An HTML file with a **div** is needed. This **div** will contain the user's typed keys. A **script** tag that points to the index.js file is also needed.

```
<html>
    <head>
    </head>
    <body>
        <div id="text">
        </div>
    </body>
    <script src="index.js"></script>
</html>
```

In index.js, add the event listener that will be used to record keystrokes. In the previous event listener example, you needed to attach the listener to the **button**. But here, location does not matter. All keystrokes should be recorded. The event listener should be added to the entire **document**.

```
// index.js
document.addEventListener('keydown', function(event) {
    console.log(event);
});
```

After refreshing the page and pressing the "a" key, the event object for a keypress can be seen in the developer console.

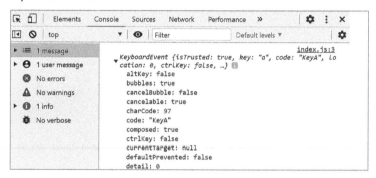

The **event** object has a ton of information, but the property **key** has the important information. It contains the name of the keystroke.

```
// index.js
document.addEventListener('keydown', function(event) {
    console.log(event.key);
});
```

With a **console.log**, the name of the key that was pressed can be seen in the developer console. When "hi my name is andrew" is typed, each individual key name will be printed out in the developer console.

After confirming that the event listener is picking up keystrokes, add the statements necessary to update the **div** with text.

```
// index.js
document.addEventListener('keydown', function(event) {
    console.log(event.key);
    var div = document.getElementById('text');
    div.innerHTML += event.key;
});
```

Pretty slick! But wait, what happens if you make a mistake and want to revert text? What happens if you hit backspace?

Wow, that's not slick at all! It looks like JavaScript records all types of keypresses. When a backspace is registered, the page should delete a character. If not, a character should be added to the existing text. Sounds like a conditional is needed, doesn't it?

You will make that and add your conditional to handle your backspace condition. That also means a character removal function needs to be written.

```javascript
function removeLastChar(str) {
    var newStr = ''
    for (var i = 0; i < str.length - 1; i++) {
        newStr += str[i];
    }
    return newStr;
}
document.addEventListener('keydown', function(event) {
    var div = document.getElementById('text');
    if (event.key === 'Backspace') {
        console.log('backspace!');
        div.innerHTML = removeLastChar(div.innerHTML);
    } else {
        div.innerHTML += event.key;
    }
});
```

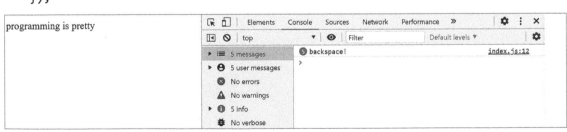

Refresh the page. Type a message. Press backspace five times. Looks like the characters are now being deleted!

Crack the Code

It's important to understand how JavaScript interacts with HTML, because you will be solving some hard (but fun) challenges soon!

1. After an HTML file is updated and saved, the browser does not immediately update. Why?
2. What is the **document** object?
3. What is the purpose of **document.getElementsByClassName** and **document.getElementById**?
4. How are **document.getElementsByClassName** and **document.getElementById** different?
5. What property contains the text inside an HTML element?
6. What is an event listener?
7. In our examples, the click event listener was applied directly to the **button**. But the keystroke event listener was applied to the entire **document**. Why?
8. What are the two ways to use the HTML **script** tag to run JavaScript code when the page loads?

Debugging

To extend the previous exercise, I want to add a **button** that will automatically destroy all text on the page. The HTML file now needs a **button**.

```html
<html>
    <head>
    </head>
    <body>
        <div id="text">
        </div>
        <button id="delete-all">
            Delete all Text
        </button>
    </body>
    <script src=" index.js"></script>
</html>
```

But something is wrong. For some reason, clicking anywhere on the page is causing the **button** to behave strangely. The text is not disappearing, either!

```
document.addEventListener('click', function() {
    var div = document.getElementById('delete-all');
    div.innerHTML = '';
});
```

CODER'S CHECKLIST » Let's review the topics we covered

You've come a long way since chapter 1, haven't you? By building the prerequisite knowledge of programming fundamentals, you are finally getting close to the work and challenges modern programmers face! Here is what you learned in this chapter.

- Basics of HTML, including tags, text on the page, and attributes
- How to run JavaScript code on page load
- The developer console
- JavaScript HTML selectors
- Modifying HTML elements using JavaScript
- Event listeners

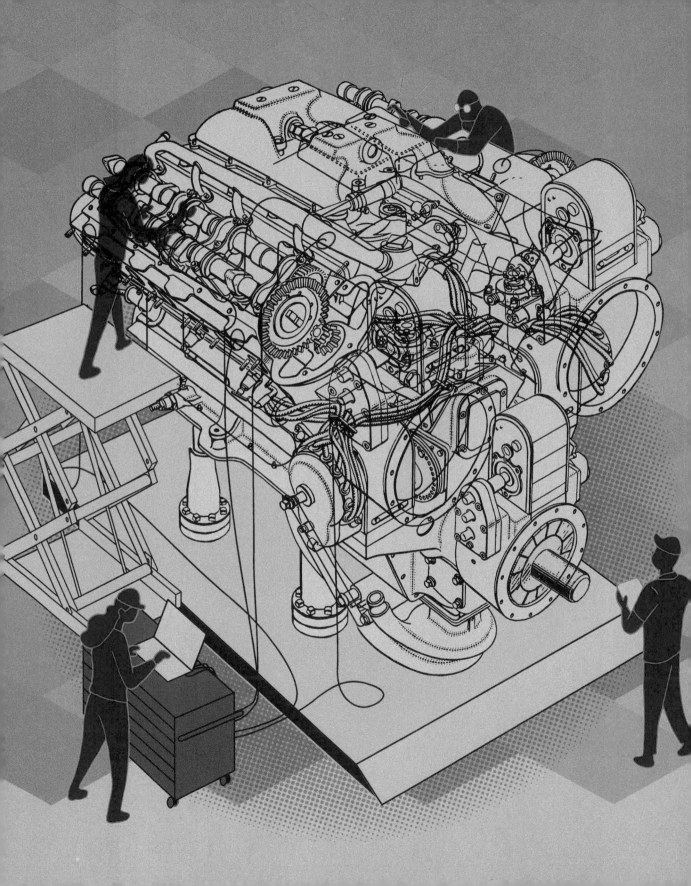

CHAPTER 10

Game Time

You made it! Your tool kit now consists of programming fundamentals, object-oriented programming, and web-specific JavaScript. You have covered all of the fundamentals that this book has to offer. That being said, what good are these lessons if you don't do anything with them? Let's wrap it up by creating a game—one that will run on the browser.

Hangman on the Browser

The game of choice is Hangman. Sure, you've made Hangman for the terminal. The fundamentals don't change. But when it comes to the browser, some parts of the implementation are tricky!

Hangman: Terminal vs. Browser

The main difference between browser and terminal are the graphics. Instead of **console.log**, HTML needs to be modified. For example, the way you decide whether a player has lost is identical.

```
Hangman.prototype.playerLost = function () {
    return this.remainingBadGuesses === 0;
};
```

On the other hand, the way guessed characters are shown is going to be completely different. On the browser, a **console.log** isn't going to cut it anymore!

```
Hangman.prototype.showGuessedCharacters = function() {
    var str = '';
    for (var i = 0; i < this.charactersGuessed.length; i++) {
        var currChar = this.charactersGuessed[i];
```

```
        str += currChar;
        str += ' ';
    }
    console.log('You have currently guessed the following characters:');
    console.log(str);
};
```

Content must be visually expressed using HTML. In the same way you need to use clever tricks to solve algorithms, you need to get creative to manipulate HTML.

Hangman Implementation

None of the rules of Hangman change. A majority of the smaller challenges from the previous chapters are the same. The difference is the implementation.

Before starting, revisit the game conditions. This is an identical template from the object-oriented programming chapter (page 93).

Variables to Track:

→ The secret word
→ Characters guessed
→ Total number of bad guesses before losing

Terminating Conditions:

→ If the player has made six bad guesses, the player has lost.
→ If the player has guessed all the characters in the secret word, the player has won.

Hangman Game Cycle:

→ Show characters that have been guessed.
→ Prompt the player to guess a character.
→ Add the guessed character to a character bank.
→ Reveal correctly guessed characters in the secret word.

Game Bounds:

→ Prevent identical guesses.
→ Prevent non-alphabetic guesses.
→ Ignore capitalization when guessing.

GAME GRAPHICS

You need to show the player what is happening while they are playing the game. Everything that was done on the terminal, with raw text, now must be done on the browser, with HTML manipulation. To do so you will implement the following rules:

1. When the game starts
   a. Blank spaces for the secret word
   b. Space to show letters that have been guessed
   c. Message bar to display game feedback to the player
   d. Hangman progress on the rope
2. When the player guesses a character
   a. If character is correct
      - Inform them using message in the message bar
      - Reveal it in the secret word section
      - Add to the list of guessed characters
   b. If character is wrong
      - Tell them using a message
      - Add a body part to the person
      - Add to the list of guessed characters
   c. If character has been previously guessed
      - Tell them using a message
      - Ignore the guess
3. Check to see if the player has won or lost
   a. If neither won or lost, continue game
   b. If won, open game over screen and tell them they won
   c. If lost, open game over screen and tell them they lost
   d. If won or lost, allow game resetting

HTML File

Before coding, an HTML file is needed, or else JavaScript would have nothing to manipulate! Here is the file in full. This is including the CSS and JavaScript imports, with `link` and `script` tags. Each part will be individually examined.

```
<html>
    <head>
        <link rel="stylesheet" href="hangman.css">
        <link rel="stylesheet" href="person.css">
    </head>
    <body>
        <div>
```

```
            <div id="rope">
                |
            </div>
            <div id="pole">
            </div>
        </div>
        <div id="person">
            <div id="head" class="appendage intact">
                o
            </div>
            <div id="torso">
                <div id="arm-left" class="appendage intact">
                    /
                </div>
                <div id="body" class="appendage intact">
                    |
                </div>
                <div id="arm-right" class="appendage intact">
                    \
                </div>
            </div>
            <div id="lower">
                <div id="leg-left" class="appendage intact">
                    /
                </div>
                <div id="leg-right" class="appendage intact">
                    \
                </div>
            </div>
        </div>
        <div id="game">
            <div id="guessed-characters">
            </div>
            <div id="secret-word">
            </div>
            <div id="game-message">
            </div>
        </div>
```

```
            <div id="game-end" class="no-display">
                <div id="game-end-message" class="end-text">
                </div>
                <div id="revealed-secret" class="end-text">
                </div>
                <button id="restart-game" class="end-text">
                    Play again
                </button>
            </div>
        </body>
        <script src="hangman.js"></script>
    </html>
```

HANGMAN PROGRESS

This is the set of elements that create your person to be hanged. All of the elements are hidden when the game starts and will progressively be revealed when the player gives incorrect guesses. Body-part revealing will be performed by removing the **class "intact"**.

```
    <div id="person">
        <div id="head" class="appendage intact">
            o
        </div>
        <div id="torso">
            <div id="arm-left" class="appendage intact">
                /
            </div>
            <div id="body" class="appendage intact">
                |
            </div>
            <div id="arm-right" class="appendage intact">
                \
            </div>
        </div>
        <div id="lower">
            <div id="leg-left" class="appendage intact">
                /
            </div>
            <div id="leg-right" class="appendage intact">
```

```
            \
          </div>
       </div>
    </div>
```

GUESSED CHARACTERS

In the terminal, `console.log` was used. This time, HTML `div` elements with the character is required. Those `div` elements will be inserted inside.

```
<div id="guessed-characters">
</div>
```

SECRET WORD

When the game starts, all of the characters will be pre-inserted into the page as `div` elements with the characters inside. JavaScript and CSS will be used to reveal them when they have been correctly guessed.

```
<div id="secret-word">
</div>
```

GAME OVER SCREEN

The game over HTML is prepared but is hidden using CSS, with the `class` "no-display". Once the game ends in a win or loss, this content will be revealed. JavaScript will be used to display a message, reveal the secret word, and give the player an option to reset the game and play again.

```
<div id="game-end" class="no-display">
    <div id="game-end-message" class="end-text">
    </div>
    <div id="revealed-secret" class="end-text">
    </div>
    <button id="restart-game" class="end-text">
        Play again
    </button>
</div>
```

CSS Game Files

As stated previously, this book won't be covering the inner workings of the CSS. So far, only the role of each `id` and `class` has been discussed. In addition to that, in order to complete the task at hand, below is all of the necessary CSS that you will need to know. Remember that the file name is important.

```css
hangman.css
body {
    width: 500px;
    height: 500px;
    border: 2px solid black;
    position: relative;
    display: flex;
    justify-content: center;
    align-items: center;
    font-family: system-ui;
    user-select: none;
}
#game {
    position: absolute;
    bottom: 0;
    width: 70%;
    min-height: 150px;
    padding: 20px;
    padding-top: 50px;
    background-color: rgba(207,
138, 70);
    display: flex;
    flex-direction: column;
    align-items: center;
}
#game-end {
    position: absolute;
    width: 250px;
    height: 150px;
    display: flex;
    justify-content: space-around;
    flex-direction: column;
    background-color: rgba(207, 138,
70, 0.99);
    padding: 40px;
    border-radius: 10px;
    align-items: center;
}
.end-text {
    font-size: 17px;
}
.no-display {
    visibility: hidden;
    pointer-events: none;
}
.hidden {
    color: transparent;
}
.secret-character {
    margin: 3px;
    width: 25px;
    height: 25px;
    display: flex;
    justify-content: center;
    align-items: center;
    font-size: 25px;
    background-color: white;
}
.secret-character-border {
    border: 2px solid white;
}
.character {
    margin-right: 10px;
}
.game-inactive {
    opacity: 0.1;
}
#guessed-characters {
    display: flex;
    flex-wrap: wrap;
    min-height: 25px;
}
```

```css
#secret-word {
    display: flex;
    flex-wrap: wrap;
}
#remaining-guesses-container {
    display: flex;
    top: 10px;
    position: absolute;
    left: 10px;
    font-size: 15px;
}
#remaining-guesses {
    margin-left: 10px;
}
button {
    border-radius: 10px;
    padding: 5px;
    font-size: 20px;
    background-color: brown;
    color: white;
}
button:hover {
    cursor: pointer;
}
#game-message {
    margin-top: 20px;
    border: 2px white solid;
    padding: 10px;
    min-height: 18px;
    width: 80%;
}
Person.css
#person {
    font-size: 25px;
    height: 186px;
    position: relative;
}
#torso, #lower {
```

```css
    display: flex;
}
#head {
    font-size: 40px;
    position: absolute;
    top: 0;
}
#torso {
    font-size: 35px;
    top: 30px;
    position: absolute;
    left: -1px;
}
#arm-left {
    margin-top: 2px;
    margin-right: -5px;
}
#arm-right {
    margin-left: -5px;
    margin-top: 2px;
}
#lower {
    font-size: 35px;
    top: 60px;
    position: absolute;
    right: -24px;
}
.intact {
    visibility: hidden;
}
#pole {
    border-right: 5px solid brown;
    border-top: 5px solid brown;
    width: 80px;
    height: 138px;
    position: absolute;
    right: 178px;
    top: 137px;
```

```
        }
#rope {
    position: absolute;
    top: 129px;
```

```
        right: 233px;
        font-size: 40px
}
```

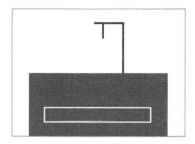

A PREVIEW

After the HTML and CSS file is prepared, your game, on the browser, should look like this!

Game CSS

CSS manipulation is a common strategy for hiding and showing elements. Here are some common ones that you'll likely put to use. If you ever get confused by what is happening when you are getting HTML elements and changing classes on them, refer back to this section!

Classes:
1. `hidden`: Hides secret character
2. `intact`: Hides body part
3. `no-display`: Hides game over screen
4. `character`: Styling for guessed character
5. `secret-character`: Styling for secret character

Game Pseudo Code

Because of the sheer complexity of game coding, this pseudo code is prepared to help us stay on track as we solve each individual challenge.

```
function initialize() {
    initialize hangman object
    insert secret word on HTML
    document.addEventListener('keydown', function (event) {
        get the key that was pressed from the event parameter
        if (the key is not alphabetic) {
            stop subsequent operations
        }
        if (the key was already guessed) {
            update game message and tell the player
            stop subsequent operations
```

```
        }
        keep track of the guessed character
        insert the character as HTML into the page
        if (the key exists in the secret word) {
            update game message and tell the player
            update the secret word to reveal the correctly guessed key
        } else {
            update game message and tell player it was the wrong key
            add a body part to the person
        }
        if (the player has won or lost) {
            show the game over HTML, including a message and reset button
        }
    });
    ResetButton.addEventListener('click', function () {
        clear game state
        start over the game
    });
}
```

Game Implementation

Now it's time to take a deep dive into the code. Don't worry. Each challenge will be solved, one by one.

HELPER FUNCTIONS

Before starting, it is helpful to write some functions that will make your life easier. Add these to the top of the JavaScript file.

includes

This **function** checks to see if a particular character exists inside a string.

```
function includes(char, string) {
    for (var i = 0; i < string.length; i++) {
        var currentStrChar = string[i];
        if (char === currentStrChar) {
            return true;
        }
    }
}
```

```
        return false;
    }
```

createDivWithText

This **function**, using JavaScript, will create a **div** element and insert text.

```
function createDivWithText(text) {
    var div = document.createElement('div');
    div.innerHTML = text;
    return div;
}
```

getRandomEntry

This **function** accepts an array and returns a random element from it. Don't sweat the details.

```
function getRandomEntry(array) {
    var randomIdx = Math.floor(Math.random() * array.length);
    return array[randomIdx];
}
```

INITIALIZE HANGMAN OBJECT

A constructor function is needed! Recall that the following elements need to be tracked:

→ The secret word
→ Characters guessed
→ Total number of bad guesses before losing

Sounds like instance variables are needed. The parameter will be a secret word. There are six bad guesses because a person has six body parts in Hangman (head, body, right arm, left arm, right leg, left leg).

```
function Hangman(secretWord) {
    this.secretWord = secretWord;
    this.charactersGuessed = '';
    this.remainingBadGuesses = 6;
}
```

But wait! How is a secret word going to be selected? Using an array of secret words, a random one can be selected using the **getRandomEntry** function. Easy, right? Here is what the **initialize** function currently looks like.

```
function initialize() {
    var wordBank = [ // add whatever words you want here!
        'cat',
        'soul',
        'watch',
```

```
    ];
    var randomWord = getRandomEntry(wordBank);
    var game = new Hangman(randomWord);
}
```

INSERT SECRET WORD INTO HTML

To add the secret word on the page, JavaScript will be used to create each **div** element and the **class** we need to style it. Another **class**, **"hidden"**, is added to hide the character.

```
Hangman.prototype.initializeSecretWord = function () {
    var container = document.getElementById('secret-word');
    for (var i = 0; i < this.secretWord.length; i++) {
        var secretChar = this.secretWord[i];
        var div = createDivWithText(secretChar);
        div.classList.add('secret-character', 'hidden');
        container.append(div);
    }
};
```

KEYDOWN EVENT LISTENER

The player will type keys and the game should react to it. A **"keydown"** event listener is needed. A majority of the game logic will be placed here!

```
document.addEventListener('keydown', function (event) {

});
```

Get the Pressed Key

The **event** parameter of the event listener contains the key that was pressed. When the player is guessing, capitalization doesn't matter, so lowercasing will be performed on the key value. All equality checks will be lowercased.

```
    document.addEventListener('keydown', function (event) {
        var guessedKey = event.key.toLowerCase();
    });
}
```

Check If the Key Is Not Alphabetic

The event listener should have no behavior if the player types a non-alphabetic key. This is the first place where we will use the `includes` function to solve a problem in an elegant manner. If the key is not alphabetic, then the event listener should halt subsequent operations.

```
Hangman.prototype.isInvalidGuess = function (guessedKey) {
    var isAlphabetic = includes(guessedKey, 'abcdefghijklmnopqrstuvwxyz');
    return !isAlphabetic;
};
```

Check If the Key Was Already Guessed

The player should not be penalized for making duplicate guesses. This check can be done using `this.charactersGuessed` to see if it is in the string of guessed characters.

```
Hangman.prototype.alreadyGuessed = function (guessedKey) {
    return includes(guessedKey, this.charactersGuessed);
};
```

Just like when the player enters a non-alphabetic key, subsequent operations will be ignored.

Print Message That Key Was Guessed

In the HTML file, there is a `div` with the `id` "game-message". This is where feedback messages will be printed on the page.

```
Hangman.prototype.updateGameMessage = function (msg) {
    var messageContainer = document.getElementById('game-message');
    messageContainer.innerHTML = msg;
};
```

The first place this method will be used is to inform the player that a previously guessed key was pressed.

Keep Track of Guessed Characters

After the user types in a key that is a valid guess, the instance variable `this.charactersGuessed` needs to be updated.

```javascript
Hangman.prototype.addToCharactersGuessed = function (char) {
    this.charactersGuessed += char;
};
```

Insert the Guessed Key on HTML

Using JavaScript, the guessed key can be inserted onto the page. The `div` that will hold these guessed characters has the `id` "`guessed-characters`".

```javascript
Hangman.prototype.appendGuessedCharacter = function (key) {
    var guessedCharDiv = createDivWithText(key);
    guessedCharDiv.classList.add('character');
    var container = document.getElementById('guessed-characters');
    container.append(guessedCharDiv);
};
```

Check If the Guessed Key Is in the Secret Word

The function `includes` makes this operation easy. Check if the guessed key has a matching character in `this.secretWord`.

```javascript
Hangman.prototype.correctGuess = function (guessedKey) {
    return includes(guessedKey, this.secretWord);
};
```

This conditional allows you to make a branching decision between a correct and an incorrect guess. A message can be printed for whether or not the player correctly guessed.

Reveal the Correct Guessed Key

If the player guessed a correct key, great! Remove the `class` "**hidden**" from that specific character. Every secret character has to be checked to see if it is a match.

```javascript
Hangman.prototype.updateSecretCharacter = function (char) {
    var allSecretChars = document.getElementsByClassName
('secret-character');
    for (var i = 0; i < allSecretChars.length; i++) {
        var secretChar = allSecretChars[i];
        if (char.toLowerCase() === secretChar.innerHTML.toLowerCase()) {
            secretChar.classList.remove('hidden');
        }
    }
};
```

Add a Body Part to the Person

If the player guessed incorrectly, they must be penalized for their foolishness. Express this visually by adding a body part to the person. The instance variable `this.remainingBadGuesses` also needs to be decremented.

Each number in `this.remainingBadGuesses` will correlate to a particular body part. A conditional chain is perfect here! The process of revealing a body part is always the removal of the **class "intact"**. The only thing that changes each time is the **id** of the HTML element. A helper function that can be reused for all of the body parts can be written. This is a much easier and cleaner approach.

```
Hangman.prototype.revealBodyPart = function () {
    this.remainingBadGuesses -= 1;
    function reveal(id) {
        var container = document.getElementById(id);
        container.classList.remove('intact');
    }
    if (this.remainingBadGuesses === 5) {
            reveal('head');
    } else if (this.remainingBadGuesses === 4) {
            reveal('body');
    } else if (this.remainingBadGuesses === 3) {
            reveal('arm-left');
    } else if (this.remainingBadGuesses === 2) {
            reveal('arm-right');
    } else if (this.remainingBadGuesses === 1) {
            reveal('leg-right');
    }                                       };
```

The game is starting to shape up!

Check If a Player Has Won or Lost

After the completion of one cycle, check to see if the game should end. Win or lose, the game should stop, and a pop-up message will appear.

The player has won if every character in `this.secretWord` exists in the `this.charactersGuessed`.

```
Hangman.prototype.playerWon = function () {
    for (var i = 0; i < this.secretWord.length; i++) {
        var secretChar = this.secretWord[i];
        if (!includes(secretChar, this.charactersGuessed)) {
            return false;
```

```
        }
    }
    return true;
};
```
The player has lost if they have no more wrong guesses.
```
Hangman.prototype.playerLost = function () {
    return this.remainingBadGuesses === 0;
};
```
This check should occur in two separate places. If the game is already over, no behavior should occur. This means we should do an early return at the very top of the event listener if the player has already won or lost. The second place is at the bottom, where we will have specific game behavior based on whether or not the game has ended.

Show Game Over HTML

If the player has won or lost, the game is over! Show them a message, as well as a button to reset the game.

This process involves revealing and hiding a lot of elements, so this is tricky. First, grey out the main game by adding the **class "game-inactive"**. After that, remove the **class "no-display"** to reveal the game over pop-up. The button will automatically be revealed.

The display message will differ based on whether the player won or lost. The method **playerLost** can be reused to check this. Another message will also reveal the secret word.

```
Hangman.prototype.showGameEnd = function () {
    var gameContainer = document.getElementById('game');
    gameContainer.classList.add('game-inactive');
    var gameEndContainer = document.getElementById('game-end');
    gameEndContainer.classList.remove('no-display');
    var messageContainer = document.getElementById('game-end-message');
    if (this.playerLost()) {
        messageContainer.innerHTML = 'You Lose!';
    } else {
        messageContainer.innerHTML = 'You Win!';
    }
    var secretContainer = document.getElementById('revealed-secret');
    secretContainer.innerHTML = 'The secret was: ' + this.secretWord;
};
```

Reset the Game on Button Click

Home stretch! The last item on your checklist is resetting the game. To reset the HTML to the initial state, you're going to use a clever little trick. First, you need to add a new instance variable to the constructor.

```
function Hangman(secretWord) {
    this.originalGameState = document.body.innerHTML;
    this.secretWord = secretWord;
    this.charactersGuessed = '';
    this.remainingBadGuesses = 6;
}
```

Before the game starts, you will be using **this.originalGameState** to store string versions of all of the HTML in the state it existed when the page first loaded. Once that is stored, resetting the game is easy. Just replace all of the game's HTML with **this.originalGameState**,

```
Hangman.prototype.resetGameState = function () {
    document.body.innerHTML = this.originalGameState;
};
```

It's great that you reset the page. But that also means all of your game logic is gone. You need to re-invoke our **initialize** function. I'll let you in on another secret: you can call a function inside another function. It's called **recursion**. But use it sparingly. An endless loop might occur if used incorrectly.

You're finally done! You have successfully converted our initialize function from pseudo code to JavaScript code! Hangman is now fully functional.

```
function initialize() {
    var wordBank = [ // add whatever words you want here!
        'cat',
        'soul',
        'watch',
    ];
    var randomWord = getRandomEntry(wordBank);
    var game = new Hangman(randomWord);
    game.initializeSecretWord();
    document.addEventListener('keydown', function (event) {
```

```javascript
        if (game.playerWon() || game.playerLost()) {
            return;
        }
        var guessedKey = event.key.toLowerCase();
        if (game.isInvalidGuess(guessedKey)) {
            return;
        }
        if (game.alreadyGuessed(guessedKey)) {
            game.updateGameMessage('You already guessed ' + guessedKey);
            return;
        }
        game.addToCharactersGuessed(guessedKey);
        game.appendGuessedCharacter(guessedKey);
        if (game.correctGuess(guessedKey)) {
            game.updateGameMessage('Yes! The secret contains '
+ guessedKey);
            game.updateSecretCharacter(guessedKey);
        } else {
            game.updateGameMessage('Nope, the secret does not have a '
+ guessedKey);
            game.revealBodyPart();
        }
        if (game.playerWon() || game.playerLost()) {
            game.showGameEnd();
            return;
        }
    });
    var playAgainButton = document.getElementById('restart-game');
    playAgainButton.addEventListener('click', function () {
        game.resetGameState();
        initialize();
    });
}
```

As a collective whole, this is what the file should look like. Remember that the file name matters!

hangman.js

```javascript
Hangman.prototype.revealBodyPart = function () {
    this.remainingBadGuesses -= 1;
    function reveal(id) {
```

```javascript
    var container = document.getElementById(id);
        container.classList.remove('intact');
    }
    if (this.remainingBadGuesses === 5){
        reveal('head');
    } else if (this.remainingBadGuesses === 4) {
        reveal('body');
    }else if (this.remainingBadGuesses === 3){
        reveal('arm-left');
    }else if (this.remainingBadGuesses === 2){
        reveal('arm-right');
    }else if (this.remainingBadGuesses === 1){
        reveal('leg-left');
    }
};
function includes(char, string) {
    for (var i = 0; i < string.length; i++) {
        var currentStrChar = string[i];
        if (char === currentStrChar) {
            return true;
        }
    }
    return false;
}
function createDivWithText(text) {
    var div = document.createElement('div');
    div.innerHTML = text;
    return div;
}
function getRandomEntry(array) {
    var randomIdx = Math.floor(Math.random() * array.length);
    return array[randomIdx];
}
function Hangman(secretWord) {
    this.originalGameState = document.body.innerHTML;
    this.secretWord = secretWord;
    this.charactersGuessed = '';
    this.remainingBadGuesses = 6;
}
```

```javascript
Hangman.prototype.playerLost = function () {
    return this.remainingBadGuesses === 0;
};
Hangman.prototype.showGameEnd = function () {
    var gameContainer = document.getElementById('game');
    gameContainer.classList.add('game-inactive');
    var gameEndContainer = document.getElementById('game-end');
    gameEndContainer.classList.remove('no-display');
    var messageContainer = document.getElementById('game-end-message');
    if (this.playerLost()) {
        messageContainer.innerHTML = 'You Lose!';
    } else {
        messageContainer.innerHTML = 'You Win!';
    }
    var secretContainer = document.getElementById('revealed-secret');
    secretContainer.innerHTML = 'The secret was: ' + this.secretWord;
};
Hangman.prototype.playerWon = function () {
    for (var i = 0; i < this.secretWord.length; i++) {
        var secretChar = this.secretWord[i];
        if (!includes(secretChar, this.charactersGuessed)) {
            return false;
        }
    }
    return true;
};
Hangman.prototype.addToCharactersGuessed = function (char) {
    this.charactersGuessed += char;
};
Hangman.prototype.appendGuessedCharacter = function (key) {
    var guessedCharDiv = createDivWithText(key);
    guessedCharDiv.classList.add('character');
    var container = document.getElementById('guessed-characters');
    container.append(guessedCharDiv);
};
Hangman.prototype.updateSecretCharacter = function (char) {
    var allSecretChars
```

```
    = document.getElementsByClassName('secret-character');
        for (var i = 0; i < allSecretChars.length; i++) {
            var secretChar = allSecretChars[i];
            if (char.toLowerCase() === secretChar.innerHTML.toLowerCase()) {
                secretChar.classList.remove('hidden');
Hangman.prototype.revealBodyPart = function () {
    this.remainingBadGuesses -= 1;
    function reveal(id) {
        var container = document.getElementById(id);
        container.classList.remove('intact');
    }
    if (this.remainingBadGuesses === 5) {
        reveal('head');
    } else if (this.remainingBadGuesses === 4) {
        reveal('body');
    } else if (this.remainingBadGuesses === 3) {
        reveal('arm-left');
    } else if (this.remainingBadGuesses === 2) {
        reveal('arm-right');
    } else if (this.remainingBadGuesses === 1) {
        reveal('leg-left');
    }
};
        }
    }
};
Hangman.prototype.renderRemainingGuesses = function () {
    var container = document.getElementById('remaining-guesses');
    container.innerHTML = this.remainingBadGuesses;
};
Hangman.prototype.resetGameState = function () {
    document.body.innerHTML = this.originalGameState;
};
Hangman.prototype.initializeSecretWord = function () {
    var container = document.getElementById('secret-word');
    for (var i = 0; i < this.secretWord.length; i++) {
        var secretChar = this.secretWord[i];
        var div = createDivWithText(secretChar);
```

```javascript
        div.classList.add('secret-character', 'hidden');
        container.append(div);
    }
};
Hangman.prototype.alreadyGuessed = function (guessedKey) {
    return includes(guessedKey, this.charactersGuessed);
};
Hangman.prototype.isInvalidGuess = function (guessedKey) {
    var isAlphabetic = includes(guessedKey, 'abcdefghijklmnopqrstuvwxyz');
    return !isAlphabetic;
};
Hangman.prototype.updateGameMessage = function (msg) {
    var messageContainer = document.getElementById('game-message');
    messageContainer.innerHTML = msg;
};
Hangman.prototype.clearGameMessage = function () {
    var messageContainer = document.getElementById('game-message');
    messageContainer.innerHTML = '';
};
Hangman.prototype.correctGuess = function (guessedKey) {
    return includes(guessedKey, this.secretWord);
};
function initialize() {
    var wordBank = [ // add whatever words you want here!
        'cat',
        'soul',
        'watch',
    ];
    var randomWord = getRandomEntry(wordBank);
    var game = new Hangman(randomWord);
    game.initializeSecretWord();
    document.addEventListener('keydown', function (event) {
        if (game.playerWon() || game.playerLost()) {
            return;
        }
        var guessedKey = event.key.toLowerCase();
        if (game.isInvalidGuess(guessedKey)) {
            return;
        }
```

```javascript
        if (game.alreadyGuessed(guessedKey)) {
            game.updateGameMessage('You already guessed ' + guessedKey);
            return;
        }
        game.addToCharactersGuessed(guessedKey);
        game.appendGuessedCharacter(guessedKey);
        if (game.correctGuess(guessedKey)) {
            game.updateGameMessage('Yes! The secret contains '
+ guessedKey);
            game.updateSecretCharacter(guessedKey);
        } else {
            game.
updateGameMessage('Nope, the secret does not have a ' + guessedKey);
            game.revealBodyPart();
        }
        if (game.playerWon() || game.playerLost()) {
            game.showGameEnd();
            return;
        }
    });
    var playAgainButton = document.getElementById('restart-game');
    playAgainButton.addEventListener('click', function () {
        game.resetGameState();
        initialize();
    });
}
initialize();
```

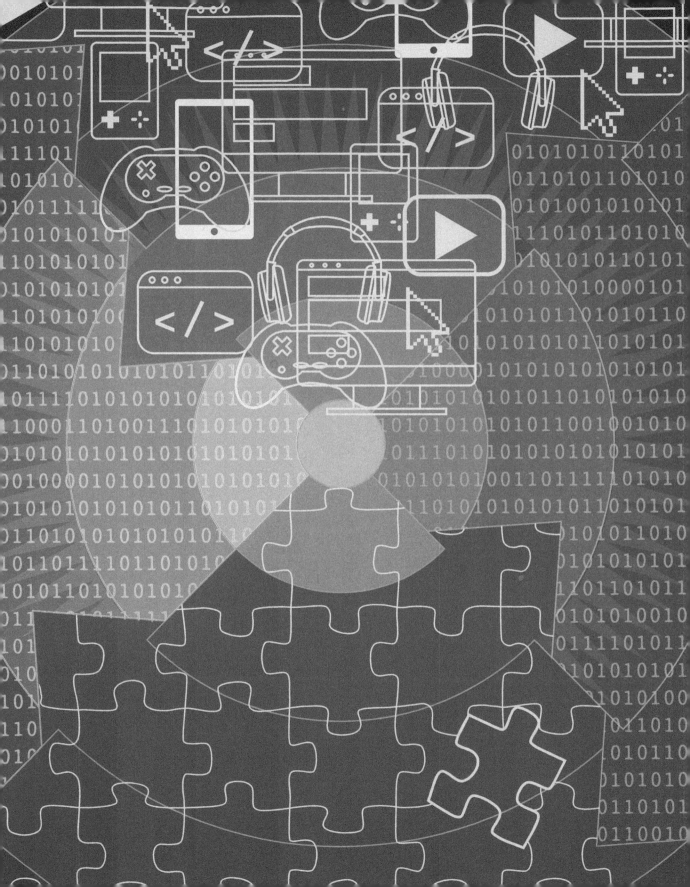

CHAPTER 11

Last Stop: Website Upgrades

Whew! The light at the end of the tunnel. You have now covered everything that has led you to the ability to develop a basic game on the browser. Now, it is time to put extra emphasis on the web development aspect of JavaScript and update an existing website. Building websites is very challenging. Not only do you need to solve algorithms, you also have to have a good understanding of how to manipulate HTML in creative ways. Ready to spruce up an existing website? Let's get started!

Incomplete To-Do List Code

Let's look at upgrading a to-do list. They're quite useful when keeping track of our daily agenda! This website has an input box that creates an entry with the text.

```
index.html
<html>
<head>
```

```html
    <link rel="stylesheet" href="index.css">
</head>
<body>
    <h2>
        Things I forget to do
    </h2>
    <div id="new-todo-container">
        <textarea id="new-todo"></textarea>
        <button id="create-button">
            Create
        </button>
    </div>
    <div id="todos">
    </div>
</body>
<script src="index.js"></script>
</html>
```

index.js

```javascript
function initPage() {
    function createParentDiv() {
        var parentDiv = document.createElement('div');
        parentDiv.classList.add('todo-container');
        return parentDiv;
    }
    function createTextDiv(text) {
        var div = document.createElement('div');
        div.innerHTML = text;
        div.classList.add('todo');
        return div;
    }
    function createEditableTextAreaWithHeight(text, height) {
        var editTextArea = document.createElement('textarea');
        editTextArea.classList.add('editing-todo');
        editTextArea.style.height = height;
        editTextArea.value = text;
        return editTextArea;
    }
    function destroyInnerContent(htmlElement) {
        htmlElement.innerHTML = '';
```

```javascript
}
function getParentDiv(htmlElement) {
    return htmlElement.parentElement;
}
function getHtmlElementHeight(htmlElement) {
    return htmlElement.offsetHeight;
}
function getTodoText(parentDiv) {
    var editableTodo = parentDiv.getElementsByClassName('editing-todo');
    var nonEditableTodo = parentDiv.getElementsByClassName('todo');
    if (editableTodo[0] !== undefined) {
        return editableTodo[0].value;
    } else {
        return nonEditableTodo[0].innerHTML;
    }
}
function createCancelButton() {
    var cancelButton = document.createElement('div');
    cancelButton.innerHTML = 'cancel';
    cancelButton.classList.add('cancel-button');
    return cancelButton;
}
function createUpdateButton() {
    var updateButton = document.createElement('div');
    updateButton.innerHTML = 'update';
    updateButton.classList.add('update-button');
    return updateButton;
}
function createEditButton() {
    var editButton = document.createElement('span');
    editButton.innerHTML = 'edit';
    editButton.classList.add('edit-button');
    return editButton;
}
function createCloseButton() {
    var closeButton = document.createElement('span');
    closeButton.innerHTML = 'x';
    closeButton.classList.add('close-button');
```

```javascript
        return closeButton;
    }
    function createTodoWithTextAndClass(text) {
        var parentDiv = createParentDiv();
        var textDiv = createTextDiv(text);
        var closeButton = createCloseButton();
        var editButton = createEditButton();
        parentDiv.append(textDiv);
        parentDiv.append(closeButton);
        parentDiv.append(editButton);
        return parentDiv;
    }
    var textarea = document.getElementById('new-todo');
    var currentText = '';
    textarea.addEventListener('input', function (e) {
        currentText = e.currentTarget.value;
    });
    var button = document.getElementById('create-button');
    button.addEventListener('click', function () {
        if (currentText === '') {
            return;
        }
        var container = document.getElementById('todos');
        var entry = createTodoWithTextAndClass(currentText);
        textarea.value = '';
        currentText = '';
        container.append(entry);
    });
}
initPage();
```

index.css

```css
body {
    display: flex;
    flex-direction: column;
    align-items: center;
    font-family: sans-serif
}
textarea {
        font-family: sans-serif
}
#todos {
    margin-top: 40px;
}
.todo-container {
        position: relative;
}
```

```css
.todo {
    border: 1px solid black;
    min-width: 500px;
    max-width: 500px;
    word-wrap: break-word;
    border-radius: 10px;
    padding: 20px;
    margin-bottom: 20px;
    min-height: 20px;
}
.todo:hover~.close-button,
.close-button:hover {
    opacity: 1;
    transition: all 300ms;
}
.todo:hover~.edit-button,
.edit-button:hover {
    opacity: 1;
    transition: all 300ms;
}
.close-button {
    position: absolute;
    border-radius: 1000px;
    border: 2px solid black;
    top: -10;
    width: 20px;
    height: 20px;
    text-align: center;
    background-color: white;
    right: -8px;
    opacity: 0;
    cursor: pointer;
    -webkit-user-select: none;
}
.edit-button {
    position: absolute;
    border-radius: 10px;
    border: 2px solid black;
```

```css
    top: 18;
    width: 25px;
    padding: 2px;
    text-align: center;
    background-color: white;
    right: -15px;
    opacity: 0;
    cursor: pointer;
    -webkit-user-select: none;
    font-size: 12px;
}
.editing-todo {
    border: 1px solid black;
    min-width: 540px;
    max-width: 540px;
    word-wrap: break-word;
    padding: 20px;
    margin-bottom: 20px;
    font-size: 16px;
    min-height: 60px;
}
.update-button {
    position: absolute;
    border-radius: 10px;
    border: 2px solid black;
    bottom: 10;
    width: 50px;
    padding: 2px;
    text-align: center;
    background-color: white;
    left: 15px;
    cursor: pointer;
    -webkit-user-select: none;
    font-size: 12px;
}
.cancel-button {
    position: absolute;
    border-radius: 10px;
```

```
    border: 2px solid black;                    #new-todo {
    bottom: 10;                                     padding: 5px;
    width: 45px;                                    width: 400px;
    padding: 2px;                                   height: 80px;
    text-align: center;                             font-size: 16px;
    background-color: white;                    }
    left: 80px;                                 #create-button:hover {
    cursor: pointer;                                cursor: pointer;
    -webkit-user-select: none;                  }
    font-size: 12px;                            #create-button {
}                                                   background-color: white;
#new-todo-container {                               border: 1px solid black;
    display: flex;                              }
}
```

NONE OF THE BUTTONS WORK

A fully functional to-do list, kind of? After hovering over an entry, a few buttons will show up. Clicking them doesn't do anything.

Things I forget to do

Wow, what a coincidence. That was definitely not set up by the author of this book! Let's use your understanding of how JavaScript can be used, in conjunction with HTML, to implement the missing features.

Helper Functions

A few helper functions have been prepared for convenience.

DESTROYINNERCONTENT

This function removes all HTML elements that are inside it.

```
function destroyInnerContent(htmlElement) {
    htmlElement.innerHTML = '';
}
```

GETPARENTDIV

This function will get the parent element of a particular HTML element. This will be used when you want to have HTML destroy itself.

```
function getParentDiv(htmlElement) {
    return htmlElement.parentElement;
}
```

GETHTMLELEMENTHEIGHT

This function will get the height of the HTML element. This will be used to manually change the height of HTML elements.

```
function getHtmlElementHeight(htmlElement) {
    return htmlElement.offsetHeight;
}
```

GETTODOTEXT

This function's parameter is the to-do entry div and will extract the text inside.

```
function getTodoText(parentDiv) {
    var editableTodo = parentDiv.getElementsByClassName('editing-todo');
    var nonEditableTodo = parentDiv.getElementsByClassName('todo');
    if (editableTodo[0] !== undefined) {
        return editableTodo[0].value;
    } else {
        return nonEditableTodo[0].innerHTML;
    }
}
```

Deleting a To-Do Entry

When the close icon is clicked, it would make perfect sense to have the entry be deleted, right? Let's do that. First, inspect how the close button is made. The function is called `createCloseButton`. Right now, the only thing this function is doing is creating a close button. But there is no behavior associated with it! It's time to add an event listener.

In order to remove a to-do entry, we need a variable that points to the parent of the close button. In the process of removing the parent from the page, this will destroy all of the content inside. Easy peasy, right?

```javascript
function createCloseButton() {
    var closeButton = document.createElement('span');
    closeButton.innerHTML = 'x';
    closeButton.classList.add('close-button');
    closeButton.addEventListener('click', function () {
        var parentDiv = getParentDiv(closeButton);
        parentDiv.remove();
    });
    return closeButton;
}
```

Editing a To-Do Entry

Are you ready for hard mode? This time, you will add the ability to update an existing to-do entry.

In order to accomplish this, you have to get clever about how you manipulate the HTML on the page.

CREATE EDITABLE TEXT

Currently, to-do entries exist as characters on the page, which can't be manipulated by a visitor to the page. But there is a special type of HTML called **textarea** that creates a textbox for users to type into.

What if you were to destroy the HTML that is holding the text, immediately insert the **textarea** in the exact same spot, insert the previous text into the **textarea**, and then style the **textarea** in the exact same way? Wouldn't it look like the **div** was somehow converted into a **textarea**?

Inside the **createEditButton** function, a click event listener is needed. This is where things get very tricky!

First, create the **textarea**. There already is a function for that, called **createEditableTextAreaWithHeight**, which takes two arguments. One is the text to pre-insert into the **textarea**. The other is the height of HTML element. In order to make it look like it magically changed to a **textarea**, the height of the **textarea** needs to be the same as the HTML element it is replacing.

```
function createEditButton() {
    var editButton = document.createElement('span');
    editButton.innerHTML = 'edit';
    editButton.classList.add('edit-button');
    editButton.addEventListener('click', function () {
        var parentDiv = getParentDiv(editButton);
        var originalText = getTodoText(parentDiv);
        var currentHTMLHeight = getHtmlElementHeight(parentDiv);
        var editingTextArea = createEditableTextAreaWithHeight(original-
Text, currentHTMLHeight);
    });
    return editButton;
}
```

After setting that up, the **div** with the uneditable text needs to be destroyed. Append the newly created **textarea**. The create and update buttons now need to be recreated and inserted into the page.

For a better user experience, a method called **focus** can be used on the **textarea** so the cursor immediately jumps into the **textarea** after the edit button is clicked. Test it out yourself now! It should change to an editable HTML element.

```
function createEditButton() {
    var editButton = document.createElement('span');
    editButton.innerHTML = 'edit';
    editButton.classList.add('edit-button');
    editButton.addEventListener('click', function () {
        var parentDiv = getParentDiv(editButton);
        var originalText = getTodoText(parentDiv);
        var currentHTMLHeight = getHtmlElementHeight(parentDiv);
        var editingTextArea = createEditableTextAreaWithHeight
(originalText, currentHTMLHeight);
        destroyInnerContent(parentDiv);
        parentDiv.append(editingTextArea);
        var updateButton = createUpdateButton();
        var cancelButton = createCancelButton(originalText);
```

```
        parentDiv.append(updateButton);
        parentDiv.append(cancelButton);
        editingTextArea.focus();
    });
    return editButton;
}
```

Updating Text After It Has Been Edited

It looks like your to-do entry magically turned into an editable element. But what good is a **textarea** if it doesn't have the ability to revert back into its uneditable state? Let's add an update button, using the function **createUpdateButton**. Right now, the button doesn't do anything. Add an event listener to change that. Before destroying the **textarea** HTML element, save the inner text to a variable.

```
function createUpdateButton() {
    var updateButton = document.createElement('div');
    updateButton.innerHTML = 'update';
    updateButton.classList.add('update-button');
    updateButton.addEventListener('click', function () {
        var parentDiv = getParentDiv(updateButton);
        var updatedText = getTodoText(parentDiv);
    });
    return updateButton;
}
```

Now you're ready to manipulate the HTML on the page. Destroy the **textarea**, recreate the un-editable to-do entry with the text inside, and insert it in the exact position the **textarea** previously was in. Pretty slick!

```
function createUpdateButton() {
    var updateButton = document.createElement('div');
    updateButton.innerHTML = 'update';
    updateButton.classList.add('update-button');
    updateButton.addEventListener('click', function () {
        var parentDiv = getParentDiv(updateButton);
        var updatedText = getTodoText(parentDiv);
        destroyInnerContent(parentDiv);
        var textDiv = createTextDiv(updatedText);
        var closeButton = createCloseButton();
        var editButton = createEditButton();
        parentDiv.append(textDiv);
        parentDiv.append(closeButton);
        parentDiv.append(editButton);
    });
    return updateButton;
}
```

Canceling Text Update

But what if the user changes their mind and wants to cancel their update? You will need a button for that. This website already has a function called **createCancelButton**. You need to add behavior to it. That means it is time for another event listener!

When hitting cancel, the text needs to revert back to its original state. But you lose the text value when the user starts typing in the **textarea**. How can this be resolved?

You need to get a little creative! This time around, add a parameter to **createCancelButton**. This parameter will store the original text inside the function.

```
function createCancelButton(originalText) {
    var cancelButton = document.createElement('div');
    cancelButton.innerHTML = 'cancel';
    cancelButton.classList.add('cancel-button');
    return cancelButton;
}
```

When the cancel button is clicked, the event listener will destroy the **textarea**, create the uneditable **div**, and reinsert the previously saved text. Give your new and improved to-do list a try.

```javascript
function createCancelButton(originalText) {
    var cancelButton = document.createElement('div');
    cancelButton.innerHTML = 'cancel';
    cancelButton.classList.add('cancel-button');
    cancelButton.addEventListener('click', function () {
        var parentDiv = getParentDiv(cancelButton);
        destroyInnerContent(parentDiv);
        var textDiv = createTextDiv(originalText);
        var closeButton = createCloseButton();
        var editButton = createEditButton();
        parentDiv.append(textDiv);
        parentDiv.append(closeButton);
        parentDiv.append(editButton);
    });
    return cancelButton;
}
```

Congratulations!

You have successfully navigated the basics of JavaScript! This book started with the raw basics, and slowly but surely you have learned enough to build a game and website in JavaScript. There were a few very challenging chapters in this book, and I congratulate you for making it across the finish line!

With all that said, your journey does not stop here. The fundamentals that have been covered in this book are just the tip of the iceberg. I hope you have had as much fun working through this book as I had writing it! I'm passionate about programming, and I sincerely hope you continue to build your skills as a coder in the coming years.

Answer Key

Chapter 3 Solutions

CRACK THE CODE

1. **When are comments useful?**
   Comments can be used for many situations. They can be used to explain what the code is doing, the purpose of the algorithm that was written, and general self notes.

2. **What is the difference between declaration and assignment?**
   Declaration is the preparation of a variable. Assignment is associating a piece of data to it.

3. **Can the word "var" be used as a variable name? Why or why not?**
   It cannot, because it is a keyword. All keywords are reserved for JavaScript to use and usually will result in a runtime error if the coder attempts to use it as a variable.

4. **What keywords were covered in this chapter?**
   The following were covered: var, true, false, null, undefined.

5. **What is the main difference between the increment operators and self-assignment operators?**
   The increment operators do not need to be assigned again (with the sign equal operator). Self-assignment is a reassignment.

6. **How are values in an array accessed?**
   They are accessed by their numeric position in the array, by index (starting at 0). This is done using the bracket operator.

7. **How are values in an object accessed?**
   They are accessed by their key name with the dot operator or bracket operator. If the bracket operator is used, the key name must be a string.

8. **What value is outputted if a nonexistent index is accessed in an array?**
   It outputs undefined.

9. **What value is outputted if a nonexistent key is accessed in an object?**
It outputs **undefined**.

10. **When is bracket notation necessary for accessing a value in an object, instead of the dot operator?**
When using a variable as the key name, the bracket notation must be used.

DEBUGGING

1. **The variable doesn't seem to change in value, despite the fact that it is being incremented.**
Self-incrementing should not be assigned.
```
var num = 0;
num++;
console.log(num); // 1
```

2. **Adding two numbers together isn't working properly.**
One of the numbers is a string. Both must be the type "number."
```
var num1 = 10;
var num2 = 2;
console.log(num1 + num2); // 12
```

3. **Trying to access your dog's name 'Max' by using the key 'pug' is outputting undefined.**
When using a variable as a key, the bracket notation has to be used.
```
var dogs = {
    pug: 'Max',
    terrier: 'Appa'
};
var myDog = 'pug';
console.log(dogs[myDog]); // 'Max'
```

4. **An attempt to access the last entry in the array is outputting undefined.**
The index 3 is out of bounds of the array. For arrays, the index starts at 0.
```
var meanPeople = ['Layna', 'Layna again', 'Layna one more time'];
console.log(meanPeople[2]); // 'Layna one more time'
```

5. **A fatal runtime error is occuring when trying to print this string.**

   There is an apostrophe in the middle of the intended message: Layna's. JavaScript thinks that the string ends there, causing a runtime error. The escape operator is needed to have a quote in the middle of the string.

   ```
   console.log('Layna\'s favorite hobby is being mean to Andrew');
   ```

Chapter 4 Solutions

CRACK THE CODE

1. **What is the difference between equality operators and strict equality operators?**
   The equality operators will use type coercion if the data types are different. Strict equality never uses type coercion.

2. **What data types can the typeof operator properly check?**
   The `typeof` operator can be used on strings, numbers, `null`, `undefined`, and `booleans`. The `typeof` operator cannot be used to check arrays and objects.

3. **What data type uses the instanceof operator for proper checking?**
   The `instanceof` operator can be used to check if a data type is an array.

4. **What is the output of the following code?**
   `false`, because `true && false` evaluates to `false` and the right-hand side is already `false`.

5. **What is the output of the following code?**
   `true`, because `!false` evaluates to `true`. The right-hand side evaluates to `false`, but the OR operator (double pipes) only requires one of the sides to be `true`.

6. **Why is array[index] !== undefined an effective way of checking to see if that index exists inside an array?**
   If an index does not exist in an array that is attempted to be accessed, the output will be `undefined`.

DEBUGGING

1. **The code is saying that the array is an object.**
   The `typeof` operator cannot be used to check if an item is an array. The `instanceof` operator has to be used.

```
var item = [];
if (item instanceof Array) {
    console.log('I am an array');
} else {
    console.log('I am not an array');
}
```

2. *Super Italian Bros Two* **has won Dr. Donkey's "Game of the Year" award more than 10 times in a row. It definitely is a masterpiece. But the code is saying otherwise.**

In the `if` conditional, the value comparator is the wrong one. It should be greater than, >, not less than, <.

```
var game = 'superItalianBrosTwo';
if (donkeysGameScores[game] > 95) {
    console.log(game + ' is a masterpiece');
} else {
    console.log(game + ' is not a masterpiece');
}
// superItalianBrosTwo is a masterpiece
```

3. **I consider a game to be a mediocre game if the score is anywhere between 30 and 80.** *The Last Defender* **was a mediocre game. But it was not a bad one. Hint: Writing out complex conditions in plain English helps!**

In the `else if` condition, the left-hand side of the AND operator is incorrect. In the buggy version, that condition states: If the score is greater than 80 and the score is greater than 30. It should read: If the score is less than 80 and the score is greater than 30.

```
var game = 'theLastDefender';
var score = donkeysGameScores[game];
if (score >= 80) {
    console.log(game + ' was a fun game');
} else if (score < 80 && score > 30) {
    console.log(game + ' was an ok game');
} else {
    console.log(game + ' was a bad game');
}
// theLastDefender was an ok game
```

Chapter 5 Solutions

CRACK THE CODE

1. **Why is a terminating condition important when working with loops?**
    A loop with a terminating statement that never evaluates to false will loop forever.

2. **When iterating over an array using a for loop, a variable, usually i, is initialized to the value 0. What is the purpose of this variable when used as part of the loop terminating condition?**
    For the terminating condition, the variable "i" is used to track the index of the loop.

3. **When iterating over an array using a for loop, a variable, usually i, is initialized to the value 0. What is its purpose when used on the array inside the loop?**
    The variable i is used to access a value inside the array.

4. **Write a table for the following loop.**

ITERATION	I	CONDITION	BREED
1	0	0 < 3	pug
2	1	1 < 3	golden retriever
3	2	2 < 3	german shepherd

5. **Write a table for the following loop.**

ITERATION	I	CONDITION	GAMER
1	0	0 < 4	super
2	1	1 < 4	smurf
3	2	2 < 4	sleepy
4	3	3 < 4	moth

6. **Write a table for the following loop. Note the nonstandard incrementor, i += 2!**

ITERATION	I	CONDITION
1	0	0 < 7
2	2	2 < 7
3	4	4 < 7
4	6	6 < 7

DEBUGGING

1. **The loop is not printing the cat breeds.**
    The terminating condition is incorrect. It needs to be `catBreeds.length`.

    ```
    var catBreeds = [
        'Maine Coon',
        'ragdoll'
    ];
    for (var i = 0; i < catBreeds.length; i++) {
        console.log(catBreeds[i]);
    }
    ```

2. **The loop is not printing the bills.**
    The comparison operator in the terminating condition is incorrect. It should be greater than, not less than.

    ```
    var bills = [1, 5, 10, 20, 50];
    for (var i = 0; i < bills.length; i++) {
        console.log(bills[i]);
    }
    ```

3. **The loop is iterating one too many times. The last value printed is** undefined.
    The terminating condition in the bad code is less than or equal to. It should be less than.

    ```
    var hangmanLetters = ['d', 'a', 'r', 'k', 's', 'o', 'u', 'l', 's'];
    for (var i = 0; i < hangmanLetters.length; i++) {
        console.log(hangmanLetters[i]);
    }
    ```

4. **The loop is not printing the cat names.**
    The initialization of **i** is incorrect. There is a declaration but no assignment to the value **0**.

    ```
    var catNames = ['Pegasus', 'Maximillion', 'Joey'];
    for (var i = 0; i < catNames.length; i++) {
        console.log(catNames[i]);
    }
    ```

5. **The loop should be skipping data if the entry in the array is a string. I am trying to use** `continue` **to skip the loop's operations prematurely. But my loop is still printing out all of the data.**
    The keyword `continue`, which is meant to skip the printing of the array entry, is below the `console.log`. It should be above it.

    ```
    var mixedDataTypes = ['a', 30, 'b', 'd', 'd', 1, 3];
    for (var i = 0; i < mixedDataTypes.length; i++) {
    ```

```
        var currData = mixedDataTypes[i];
        if (typeof currData === 'string') {
            continue;
        }
        console.log(currData);
    }
```

Chapter 6 Solutions

CRACK THE CODE

1. **What qualities make functions desirable to use when programming?**
    Functions are a good way of abstracting out complex algorithms. This makes the code easier to understand. Functions are also reusable. Common operations can be pulled out into their own functions and used many times. Code that is reusable and easy to understand are qualities of well-written code.

2. **What keyword does a function need to have in order to output a value that is exposed outside of the function?**
    The keyword **return** is required.

3. **What does a function output if there is no explicit return?**
    A function with no **return** keyword outputs **undefined**.

4. **What is scope?**
    Scope is the rules of variable availability within code.

5. **What type of scope does JavaScript use? In your own words, explain what it is.**
    JavaScript uses lexical scoping. Variables that are declared inside a function are available within that function and functions inside it. Variables are never available outside of the function it is declared in.

DEBUGGING

includes
The early **return** statement condition is wrong. It should be a strict equality check. Not a strict inequality.
```
function includes(arrOrStr, item) {
    for (var i = 0; i < arrOrStr.length; i++) {
        var currItem = arrOrStr[i];
```

```
        if (currItem === item) {
            return true;
        }
    }
    return false;
}
    test('includes #1', includes('cat', 'a'), true);
    test('includes #2', includes('cat', 't'), true);
    test('includes #3', includes('cat', 'f'), false);
```

createHint

In the **else** block, it should not be an assignment. The purpose of this function is to incrementally build up a string, but using an equal sign overwrites all of the previous construction of the string. It should be an addition self-assignment.

```
function createHint(actualName, allUserGuesses) {
        var output = '';
    for (var i = 0; i < actualName.length; i++) {
        var currChar = actualName[i];
        if (includes(allUserGuesses, currChar)) {
                output += currChar + ' ';
        } else {
                output += '_ ';
        }
    }
    return output;
}
    test('createHint #1', createHint('charlie', 'chle'), 'c h _ _ l _ e ');
    test('createHint #2', createHint('cat', ''), '_ _ _ ');
    test('createHint #3', createHint('cat', 'a'), '_ a _ ');
```

correctlyGuessed

This function is checking to see if every character in **actualName** exists inside **allUserGuesses**. If the **currChar** does not exist inside the string of all of the player's guesses, we immediately know that the game is not over, and the loop can be stopped. But it should be the opposite, which requires the bang operator.

```
function correctlyGuessed(actualName, allUserGuesses) {
    for (var i = 0; i < actualName.length; i++) {
        var currChar = actualName[i];
        if (!includes(allUserGuesses, currChar)) {
```

```
            return false;
        }
    }
    return true;
}
    test('correctlyGuessed #1', correctlyGuessed('charlie', 'chle'), false);
    test('correctlyGuessed #2', correctlyGuessed('cat', 'tac'), true);
    test('correctlyGuessed #3', correctlyGuessed('cat', 'cat'), true);
```

isMultiCharGuess
Checking if a guess is multiple characters should be checking if the length is not equal to 1.

```
function isMultiCharGuess(guess) {
    return guess.length !== 1;
}
    test('isMultiCharGuess #1', isMultiCharGuess('a'), false);
    test('isMultiCharGuess #2', isMultiCharGuess('av'), true);
    test('isMultiCharGuess #3', isMultiCharGuess('c'), false);
```

Chapter 7 Solutions

CRACK THE CODE

1. **After this code is run, is players an array with 'smurf' and 'ANS' in it? Why or why not?**
    Both names exist. The shift operation removes the first entry in the array, which is 'super'.

2. **What is mutability? What data types are mutable?**
    Mutability is the concept of modifying a piece of data without creating a new version of it. Objects and arrays are mutable. All other data types are immutable.

3. **Why does string modification require a reassignment, when array and object modification do not?**
    In JavaScript, strings are immutable. In order to create a new string with two combined values, a type of assignment has to be used.

4. **What array methods decrease the size of an array?**
    The methods shift and pop remove entries in an array. They remove an entry in front and back, respectively.

5. **What array methods increase the size of the array?**

   The methods `unshift` and `push` add entries to an array. They add an entry in the front and back, respectively.

6. **Draw a table for the following function. Write what `array` will look like on each iteration and `array.length > 0`.**

ITERATION	I	CONDITION	ARRAY
1	0	5 > 0	[10, 20, 12, 30, 25]
2	1	4 > 0	[10, 20, 12, 30]
3	2	3 > 0	[10, 20, 12]
4	3	2 > 0	[10, 20]
5	4	1 > 0	[10]

7. **What is the output of the following code? Draw a table if necessary.**

ITERATION	I	CONDITION	NEWSTR
1	0	0 < 6	'a'
2	1	1 < 6	'ab'
3	2	2 < 6	'abc'
4	3	3 < 6	'abcd'
5	4	4 < 6	'abcde'
6	5	5 < 6	'abcdef'

8. **In your own words, describe what the purpose of this function is. Why does it work for both strings and arrays? Draw a table for each sample function invocation.**

   This function checks to see if a particular entry, `item`, exists inside the array or string, `arrOrStr`. It works for arrays and strings because strings can be accessed by its index in the same way arrays can.

9. **What is the value of `count`?**

   The value of `count` is 2. The variable `count` is declared in the outer scope of the function. So `increment` is directly manipulating that variable.

DEBUGGING

playersAboveSkill
The accumulator **skilledPlayers** should start as an empty array. The condition inside the loop is incorrect, for two reasons. The first is that the string variable **"skill"** cannot be used with the dot operator. Either bracket notation or the key value with the dot operator must be used. Also, it is checking if the player has less than the minimum skill requirement. It should be greater than. The **push** operation should be pushing a single player in, by accessing a player by its index.

```
function playersAboveSkill(players, skill) {
    var skilledPlayers = [];
    for (var i = 0; i < players.length; i++) {
        if (players[i].skill > skill) {
    skilledPlayers.push(players[i]);
        }
    }
    return skilledPlayers;
}
```

playerAboveAge
The object access syntax is incorrect. Because the key is a variable, the dot operator cannot be used. The bracket syntax has to be used. Again, the comparator is incorrect. It should be greater than. The **push** operation should be pushing a player in, by accessing its index.

```
function playersAboveAge(players, age) {
    var agedPlayers = [];
    for (var i = 0; i < players.length; i++) {
            var objectKey = 'age';
        if (players[i][objectKey] > age) {
    agedPlayers.push(players[i]);
        }
    }
    return agedPlayers;
}
```

`playerAboveSkillAndAge`

Nothing is wrong with this function! The only reason the output was incorrect was because the first two functions had errors in it.

```
function playerAboveSkillAndAge(players, skill, age) {
    var skilledPlayers = playersAboveSkill(players, skill);
    var skilledAndAgedPlayers = playersAboveAge(skilledPlayers, age);
    return skilledAndAgedPlayers;
}
```

Chapter 8 Solutions

CRACK THE CODE

1. **Define what an object data structure is.**
   An object data structure is a data type that can hold any number of values. They are stored as key-value pairs inside it.

2. **Define what an object is in object-oriented programming.**
   An object is an entity that holds data and functions inside it. It is a way of designing code to abstract out many operations to make code easier to understand and reason about.

3. **What variable is available across all methods?**
   Instance variables, which are assigned as a key-value pair to `this`, are available across all methods of an object.

4. **What is the syntax to invoke a method inside another method?**
   It is `this.methodName`.

5. **What is the syntax to make a constructor?**
   Functions can be used as a constructor to initialize an object instance.

6. **What is an object instance?**
   An object instance is a unique entity of an object. It personally holds all of its own data from other instances.

7. **What is the syntax to initialize an object instance?**
   The keyword `new` in front of the function invocation creates an object instance.

DEBUGGING

ChatProgram.prototype.message

The instance variable `this.chatLog` is not a function. It is an array that should have messages added to it. It is missing the **push** method.

```
ChatProgram.prototype.message = function (person, message) {
    var messageEntry = {
        person: person,
        message: message
    };
    this.chatLog.push(messageEntry);
};
```

ChatProgram.prototype.parseMessageEntry

There is no **chat** key in the message object. The text in the chat entry is in the key **message**.

```
ChatProgram.prototype.parseMessageEntry = function (chatEntry) {
        return chatEntry.person.name + ': ' + chatEntry.message;
};
```

ChatProgram.prototype.getLog

The array method **pop** is the wrong method for adding entries to an array. It should be **push**. When calling a method inside another method, `this.prototype.parseMessageEntry` should be `this.parseMessageEntry`.

```
ChatProgram.prototype.getLog = function () {
    var parsedMessages = [];
    for (var i = 0; i < this.chatLog.length; i++) {
        var chatEntry = this.chatLog[i];
        var parsedMessage = this.parseMessageEntry(chatEntry);
        parsedMessages.push(parsedMessage);
    }
    return parsedMessages;
};
```

ChatProgram.prototype.printLog

The method `this.getLog` isn't being invoked.

```
ChatProgram.prototype.printLog = function () {
    var allMessages = this.getLog();
    for (var i = 0; i < allMessages.length; i++) {
        console.log(allMessages[i]);
    }
};
```

Chapter 9 Solutions

CRACK THE CODE

1. **After an HTML file is updated and saved, the browser does not immediately update. Why?**
   The browser currently has an older version of the HTML file loaded. Refreshing the page will update it.

2. **What is the document object?**
   The **document** object is JavaScript's representation of the HTML page.

3. **What is the purpose of document.getElementsByClassName and document.getElementById?**
   These functions are used to have JavaScript point to and manipulate HTML elements on the page.

4. **How are document.getElementsByClassName and document.getElementById different?**
   document.getElementsByClassName searches for all instances of the particular class that is being searched for and returns an array-like data structure. document.getElementById, on the other hand, finds only one.

5. **What property contains the text inside an HTML element?**
   The JavaScript property that contains text is innerHTML.

6. **What is an event listener?**
   An event listener is a JavaScript function that is invoked once and then waits for a particular interaction with the page to occur. This can range from key presses to button clicks. Once an interaction occurs, JavaScript will run the code inside the second argument, the function.

7. **In our examples, the click event listener was applied directly to the button. But the keystroke event listener was applied to the entire document. Why?**
   The event should be on the button, because the event to be observed is a click on it. A click event listener on the **document** would fire if the user clicks anywhere on the page. Keystrokes, on the other hand, were not specific to a particular HTML element on the page. As long as the user is on the page, we want to invoke behavior.

8. **What are the two ways to use the HTML `script` tag to run JavaScript code when the page loads?**

The HTML `script` tag can have JavaScript code wrapped inside it. It can also be used to import JavaScript code a .js file, with the attribute `src`.

DEBUGGING

The event listener is appended to the wrong element. Adding the event listener to the **document** will invoke the behavior on any click. It has to be on the **button**. Also, the event handler is not selecting the correct **id**. The text to be cleared is inside the **div** with the **id** that is 'text'.

```
var button = document.getElementById('delete-all');
button.addEventListener('click', function() {
    var div = document.getElementById('text');
    div.innerHTML = '';
});
```

Glossary

abstraction: The concept of making a complex operation easy to use by hiding its implementation details

accumulator: A classification of a variable that is used to slowly build up a value in a loop

AND operator: The key symbol, **&&**, that requires both values to be true in order to evaluate to true

arithmetic assignment: The syntax to mathematically self-operate or self-combine strings together

array: A data structure that holds data; the data is accessed by index

assignment: The process of associating a piece of data to a variable

boolean: A data type that represents true or false

bracket notation: The syntax to access a value in an object data structure by key; also used to access a value in an array by index

break: A keyword in a loop that exits the loop entirely

camelCase: First word lowercased, with subsequent words capitalized

comment: Text written in code that is not executed

compiler: A program that analyzes and packages large groups of code at once

concat: The process of combining two arrays or strings; short for "concatenation"

conditional statement: A statement that evaluates to true or false

constructor function: A function that is the initializer of an object instance, using the keyword **new**

continue: A keyword in a loop that stops all subsequent operations and moves on to the next iteration of the loop

convention: The community's coding style that is agreed upon

CSS: Cascading style sheets, a styling language that visually enhances HTML

data structure: An umbrella term that refers to data types that hold an arbitrary amount of data

declare: The creation of a variable

decrement: Decreasing the value of a variable, whose data type is a number, by 1

document: The variable inside the browser that is JavaScript's representation of the entire website

dot operator: The syntax to access a value in an object data structure by key; also, the syntax to access an instance variable or method in an object instance

escape character: Used in strings; a special character, backslash, denotes that a key symbol should be ignored and be treated as a string

equality operator: Operator that compares whether or not two pieces of data are identical in value; equality operators use type coercion

event listener: A function that is created and waits in the background for some type of user interaction

for loop: A type of loop that will continue running until its terminating condition evaluates to false; in its syntax it also contains an initialization and after clause, for convenience

function: An entity that can be used to group statements together; the code is ready to execute on an as-needed basis

high-level language: A programming language that closely resembles human operations and logic

HTML: Hypertext markup language; a templating language that renders content in a web browser

HTMLCollection: The array-like data structure that is returned from `getElementsByClassName`

if . . . else if . . . else statement: A feature that allows conditional execution of code

immutable: A piece of data that cannot be modified

increment: Increasing the value of a variable, whose data type is a number, by 1

index: The position of an entry in an array; in JavaScript, array indexes start at 0

instance variable: A variable held inside an object instance, as a property of it; it is accessed using the bracket or dot operator

interpreter: A program that analyzes code line by line

invoke: The process of running a function, using the parenthesis syntax

keyword: Special character (and groups of characters) that is reserved for JavaScript

length: The number of entries in an array

lexical scope: Variables are available within the function they are declared in, as well as the scopes within it

link tag: The HTML tag that is used to run code from a CSS file

loop: A feature of programming languages that allows repeated execution of code

method: A function that is stored within an object; methods can only be accessed by the object instance

number: A data type in JavaScript; represents a number

NaN: The number type that represents a number that has an illogical value

NOT operator: The key symbol !, which inverses a boolean value

object: 1) A data structure that holds data in the form of key-value pairs; 2) An entity that holds data and functions within itself

object instance: An object entity that holds its own data within itself; those values are not shared among other object instances

object-oriented programming: A feature of some programming languages that empowers a programmer with the ability to create entities that internally hold their own functions and data

OR operator: The key symbol ||, which requires at least one value to be true in order to evaluate to true

parameter: Variables that are created for a function whose values can be passed when the function is invoked

pascal case: First letter of every word capitalized

property: A piece of data (including a method) that is accessible by key; applies to object data structures and object instances

pseudo code: A computer algorithm written in plain English

relational operator: An operator that compares the value between two pieces of data

scope: The rules of where variables and functions are available for use within the code

script tag: The HTML tag that is used to run code from a JavaScript file

strict equality operator: An operator that compares equality but never uses type coercion

string: The data type that represents characters

type coercion: JavaScript's process that attempts to reconcile illogical operations by changing data types for the duration of evaluation

unit testing: The process of writing tests for individual parts of a program

variable: A name that can be associated with a piece of data

while loop: A type of loop that will continue running until its terminating condition evaluates to `false`

Resources

WEBSITES

LeetCode (*LeetCode.com*) is an online bank of coding questions. They have practice questions for coders of all skills levels.

The Modern JavaScript Tutorial (*JavaScript.info*) is a high-level overview of aspects of JavaScript. This is a personal favorite, but it is not for the faint of heart!

Mozilla MDN Web Docs (*Developer.Mozilla.org/en-US*) provides comprehensive documentation for JavaScript and web development. It's very detailed and mostly used by professionals.

Stack Overflow (*StackOverflow.com*) is a community-driven help forum for coders. An overwhelming majority of questions you have about programming has been answered by someone on this site!

BOOKS

Clean Code: A Handbook of Agile Software Craftsmanship, by Robert C. Martin, is an advanced guide on coding style. Keep this one handy. If you take the time to learn about everything JavaScript has to offer, this is the way to take your ability as a programmer to the next level.

Index

JavaScript (*continued*)
event listeners, 121–123
running in HTML, 118–119
script tag importing in HTML, 120–121

K

Key-value pairs, 25
Keywords
boolean, 23
break, 53
continue, 52–53
null, 23
return, 61–62
undefined, 23–24
var, 19–20

L

Less than operators, 37
Lexical scope, 63–64
Logical operators, 37–38
Loops
in action, 54–55
debugging exercise, 56–57
defined, 4, 47
for, 51–52
modifying keywords, 52–53
while, 48–51

M

Mac setup, 9–10
Methods, 80, 94, 95, 108–110
Mutation, 82–83

N

NaN (Not a Number), 21–22
Node.js, 8, 9, 10
NOT operator, 38
Null, 23
Numbers, 20, 23, 79

O

Object-oriented programming, 60, 96–101
Objects, 25–26
as entities, 93–94
implementation, 94–96
manipulations, 81
open tag, 104
Operators
equality, 35–36, 38
instanceof, 39
logical, 37–38
relational, 37
typeof, 39
OR operator, 37
Outer scope, 63–64

P

Parameters, 61
parseFloat, 79
parseInt, 79
Pascal case, 94
pop, 81
printLog, 99
Programming, 1
Programs, 2
Properties, 25, 94, 95
Prototype, 95
Pseudo code, 5
push, 81

R

Reassignment, 19
Red squiggles (errors), 10–11
Refreshing, 107
Relational operators, 37
Replacement, 82
Runtime, 8

S

Scope, 62–64
Semicolons, 17–18

shift, 81
Statements, 17
Strict equality operator, 36
Strict inequality operator, 36
Strings, 22-23
   concatenating, 62
   immutability of, 83
   manipulations, 80
Syntax, 5

T

Terminal, 7, 9
Terminating conditions, 48
Text editors, 7-8
To-do list website upgrade, 157-168
toLowerCase, 80
toUpperCase, 80
Type coercion, 24
typeof operator, 39

U

Undefined, 23-24
Unit testing, 72-76
unshift, 81

V

Variables, 3, 18-20, 27-32, 108
VS Code, 7-8, 10, 10-14

W

Web browsers, 105-109, 126-129
Websites
   programming languages, 2-3
   upgrading, 157-168
While loops, 48-51
Windows setup, 8-9, 11-14

Acknowledgments

Thank you to Jae Bradley, a stellar colleague. He and his passion inspired me to push my boundaries and strive to be the best version of myself.

About the Author

 **Andrew Yueh** is a professional software developer who specializes in JavaScript and modern website technologies. He holds a master's degree in engineering from Texas A&M University, where his thesis cemented his passion for web development.

Andrew has worked at multiple tech companies. He served as a technical lead of a team at Wells Fargo, where he mentored multiple developers to improve their programming ability.

In his off hours, he tutors high school students in various subjects, including JavaScript fundamentals. As a hobbyist programmer, he also works on multiple personal coding projects, all written in JavaScript.